after hello

after

How to Build a Book of Business,
One Conversation at a Time

hello

Deb Feder

SUMMIT PRESS
Publishers

Printed in the United States of America
First Printing, 2022
ISBN: 9798985054668

Summit Press Publishers
PO Box 1356
Intervale, New Hampshire 03845

For information about special discounts available for bulk purchase, workshops, retreats, and webinars associated with this book or offered by Deb Feder, please contact us at hello@debfeder.com.

To my kids: Just remember that bravery is always rewarded.

To Jules and Michael: Thank you for raising the bar at the dinner table all those years.

Table of Contents

So Much for Convenience 1

Activity: The Starting Line 11

Step 1: Clear the Clutter from the Path 13

A Word on Being a Lawyer 15

The Dead-End Game of Blame and Complain . . . 19

Ditch the Daily Scramble 35

Be Brave 51

Confidently Own Your Spot at the Table 65

Stop Looking for a Way Out 73

Know and Own Your Value 83

Step 2: Know Thyself and Others 89

A Word on Conversations 91

You Before Them 95

The Myth of the Ideal Client 107

Start with What You've Got 117

Decide to Be Interested and Interesting 123

Take One Step into the Room 137

Make the First Move 147

Curiosity Leads to Clients 159

Test, Trial, Tweak 175
Step 3: 30 Conversations in 30 Days 181
30 Conversations in 30 Days 183
One More Thing 201
Acknowledgments 205
About the Author 207

So Much for Convenience

Building a book of business—a practice filled with your ideal clients—is harder now than it once was. The story of private law practice used to be work hard, be responsive, and the clients and kingdom will be yours one day.

But the story has changed.

Back in 1999, when I graduated from law school, there was no tech-friendly way to work from home. We spent long hours congregating around tables that seemed to stretch for miles, in conference rooms that, while different, always managed to feel the same. We were introduced to clients and brought along to meetings and pitches; before we knew it, we had learned the basics of building a law practice and caring for clients, simply by being around the action.

We also learned the style of the attorneys around us—the loud closer, the planner, the methodical strategist, the quiet genius, the gregarious rainmaker . . . you get the picture. By being in the mix, working with others, and paying attention, the seeds for how we'd grow our own practice were planted.

Then, technology came along and changed how we interacted with each other and our clients. Internet speeds got faster; laptops replaced desktops; cell phones turned into smartphones—and just like that, our lives started to function at the speed of our technology. With emails replacing snail-mail and faxes, our work became more flexible, and we moved away from those conference rooms more and more. Now we can practice anywhere, without a commute. And let's face it . . . it's kind of awesome. Yet, without even knowing it, we made a trade. All this flexibility no longer comes with automatic connection, and therefore requires intentional interaction.

Now, for many of you, this may seem like tales from the Dark Ages because you've only ever known a high-tech legal practice. Being comfortable with tech is a blessing and a curse; for no matter the comfort level, all this advancement and speed is leaving us all scrambling. And the more we scramble, the harder it is to spot the opportunities standing right in front of us.

Being in a room with the team allowed us to bounce ideas off one another. Without these moments, instead of feeling the power and support of a team, we now feel an intense pressure to figure everything out alone. Facing a barrage of emails and requests coming at us from all angles, at all hours, each needing an answer, we feel isolated as hell as we try to stay afloat.

In this new age, simple decisions can be elusive, and complicated ones get pushed out by the fear of making the wrong move. We avoid setting boundaries with clients and colleagues because that requires us to decide what we believe in or stand for. We have zero time to sift through our own thoughts, let alone create interesting content that spotlights our experience and expertise in a way that attracts clients, whether through the firm blog, social media, or webinars.

We hold off building a book of business because it requires us to know with whom we want to work and that we have the time to take on one more thing. We're so used to reacting for others that when asked to make meaningful decisions for ourselves, we don't know where to begin.

Here's what I know:

- All the newfound flexibility leaves you out of the conversations needed to start bringing in those big clients.
- Disconnection from clients and colleagues leaves you skittish about putting yourself out there for clients and new opportunities, especially anything substantial.
- Racing after clients, deals, cases, and the billable hour is exhausting.
- Running on fumes, instincts shot, doesn't help anybody

think through anything with clarity or confidence.

- The long hours of a law practice feel isolating, lonely, and exhausting.

There's a story you tell yourself about building a different kind of practice—one with incredible clients who simply want you and your expertise. There are no frantic, early morning emails; they simply ask for a thorough job done right. You jump into the work knowing you and your all-star team can hit a homerun.

Just imagine it—happy clients; time to give the work your full attention; projects that fall into your sweet spot; super simple business development. A great practice. A wonderful life. And a bright path in front of you.

It turns out this little fantasy is closer to reality than you might suppose. You can build a book of business that allows you to have the career and life you want. And it happens by engaging in curious, confident conversations.

That's it.

Now I know this wish is crowded out with a laundry list of complaints, exacerbated by the sheer exhaustion and frustration of a private practice. Rather than building a book of business, you are sitting on the sideline, scrambling for everyone else, excusing yourself from the action. Because there's another story playing out in your head . . .

- All the good clients are already working with someone they like. Since there's no way to get origination, I'll never grow a good practice.

- If I'm always the one to take care of others' problems, I have zero time to even think about client relationships. They should be happy I'm getting the work done.

- The good clients go to the good old boys.

- Clients who only email in the middle of the night must have sadistic expectations of working hours. Why would I want more of that?

- There are zero hours left in the day for business development (let alone self-care, families, or fun).

- No one else gets how the clients like it done, so guess who is staying up late to make it right?

On and on the story goes . . .

Yet here you are, looking for a way to renew your energy in your legal practice and bring in outstanding clients; so, bear with me. I'm here to help you build an intentional book of business.

Together we're going to find the clients and projects that light you up.

This book is going to show you how to fill your practice with clients who:

- Respect you and the demands they are asking.
- Pick you because of your expertise, and your unique approach as their trusted advisor to every deal, case, and strategy session.
- Send over project after project that fall into your sweet spot.
- Spread your name like confetti at a parade, making sure others know you're the one to call.

How It's done: Curious, Confident Conversations

1. Curiosity. Learn how to double down and pay attention, read the room, understand the nuances presented, and let your smarts shine by asking the right questions.
2. Confidence. Own your expertise, education, experience, and value. It brings a different level of energy to your work. It also allows you to see the work—including how you get it done—with greater clarity. Your secret spice:

being able to pair this new confident mindset with strategic conversations. Turns out confidence is contagious.

3. Conversations. Have simple, consistent conversations—in person (from working lunches to neighborhood BBQs), via email, LinkedIn, or networking events. You get to choose the type of conversation that works best for you; it's your vehicle to getting what you want: a book of business.

There's no order to these components. Each one is vital to the equation and plays off the other. Each one allows client relationships to be simple, without unnecessary frustration. And when your career is built off your expertise and knowledge, these same principles apply to building incredible client relationships whether you are a lawyer or not.

When you connect and relate to others, you can build the practice you want. When you have your desired book of business, you can build the kind of life you want, despite the demands of modern practice.

But it takes deconstructing your career and rethinking how you show up and engage in the conversations happening around you. All with a focus on one thing: reading the room and finding your place.

So, before engaging in these conversations, there's a mess to clean up, most of which is not of your making: the crush of information and communications, the fear of making the wrong move, and the exhaustion born of having to figure out one more thing at an inhuman pace.

You've also got to address the energy and work product you bring to the table, decide where and how to invest your time, and focus on what I like to call "showing up how you want to be seen." This means delivering excellent work in such a way that clients and colleagues trust you and your capabilities. Namely, it's building your reputation.

Why You Might Want to Listen to Me

After fifteen years of practice, and over a decade of coaching and consulting attorneys, professionals, and business owners, I firmly believe that a hyper-focused, extreme-driven, forced plan to go out there and bring in business isn't going to lead to a practice filled with clients you actually want. Instead, I'm all about the blend—using incredible conversations to attract clients, managing your days and workload, exceeding client expectations, and making it work without the new growth sucking up every moment of your life. The truth is the smallest tweaks often make the biggest difference. And, like that, the big wins come rolling in.

I've worked with attorneys and professionals in firms and organizations of all sizes, and know these things to be true:

1. Living in fire-fighting mode and jumping at every client gets you nowhere.

2. Those who understand how to manage conversations, rather than simply react to them, are winning.

3. Authentically strong relationships bring in far better business than big networks.

4. Building a book of business is not a long game, but a strategic one.

5. All of this is a choice you make every, single day.

What to Expect

In this book, you're going to find simple, actionable strategies that shift your gaze from down at the stack of work and backward in regret, to up and forward on your path to finding and keeping amazing clients. The keys to success are in your hands.

It is not easy, but it is simple. It requires that you:

1. Master your mindset. Understand that just working long hours is not the answer.

2. Play a different game. Learn how to pace your efforts and practice, so you can build solid relationships while doing the work.

3. Engage in excellence. Change how you tackle each meaningful interaction; double down on bringing value to the table and provide excellence to every client through incredible conversations and a curious mindset. It also goes without saying, you must know your stuff and keep those legal skills sharp because clients want to hire someone who's good.

In addition to the action items you'll find throughout this book, I've also put together a Guide with specific exercises I take my clients through to get them even faster results. You can access it at debfeder.com/guide (and look for footnotes throughout the book that will remind you to use it).

The first step on the path to success is when you realize long hours and scrambling for everyone else isn't going to build a magical book of business—that following the rules of the pack, and hoping it works out is more of a fool's choice than anything else. And we know that you're no fool.

With that, let's get started.

Activity: The Starting Line

[Let's Start Using the Guide][1]

Your expertise was born from experience. While you may forget what it entails, it's simple enough to retrace your steps and remind yourself. It also pays to glance in the rearview mirror to buttress your confidence because you know your stuff for a whole lot of reasons.

That's why it's important to put together a timeline of all the moments that helped shape you into the professional you are today.

This timeline of experiences is more than a resume written on a line. It's a source of valuable information about you. From it you will pull your likes and dislikes, not just in subject matter

[1] Remember, you can download the Guide at debfeder.com/guide. I will keep reminding you. But, seriously, go grab it and use it as you make your way through the book. Trust me. It's the difference between this book gathering dust on the bookshelf, and you moving the needle forward.

and projects, but with the people you work with and for. You must understand where you are energized, and where you would rather swim with sharks than spend one more minute. Once you do, you can figure out the best path to attract the clients that have you salivating from the sidelines right now.

You will refer to this timeline repeatedly. Consider it your own mini brag book. Also, a solid reminder of the fact that you didn't jump from taking the LSAT to being a partner without some significant steps in between.

Once you tap into your history—your timeline—and how you got here, you can begin moving forward.

Where to start? Your first job ever. Babysitting. Mowing lawns. Delivering pizzas. It all counts. The stories that surround a first job often give the energy of much simpler times, which makes it easier to remember why you loved (or didn't love) it.

The following chapters will cue you to add more milestones and stops to your timeline. A timeline is a work in progress. You are never done.

And in this case, the next phase is all about you finding and keeping the clients you love to work with that keep hiring you and referring you work. On repeat.

With that, let's get started on that timeline.

Step 1:

Clear the Clutter from the Path

A Word on Being a Lawyer

Great clients can't fix everything.

Being a lawyer is hard. The hours, expectations, and amount of energy it takes to succeed in this profession are legit. Nothing in this book discounts the hustle and grit it has taken to get to the point you are right now.

This profession has challenges, above and beyond the daily grind. Depending on your circumstances, you might be confronting antiquated hierarchical structures, billable hours and competing origination credit battles, and institutional bias—each a complicated and serious issue, but often layered together. Throw in the alphabet soup of additional grievances and serious wrongs and finding a way to blend the practice with real-life seems almost impossible on a good day.

Whether sleep deprivation combined with the significant quest for perfection, the impact of an intense, high-stress workload and flexible hours to get the deals and cases done is a hot storm to grapple with. With that…

1. It is important that you are healthy and working in a healthy environment. Before you do one more thing, like add a bunch of clients to the roster, make sure you are in a good mindset and healthy space to be shifting stuff around in your practice. There are resources available to support you and your mental health. The state bar associations have now set up mental health hotlines and support systems for lawyers. Please reach out and ask for help if you are struggling with your mental health and handling the pressures of practicing law.

2. Clients are paying for clarity of thought. This means you come to the table having taken care of yourself, ready to show up and think. At its most basic level, this means you are rested (yup, I mean you have slept) and can remember the last meal you had (and, preferably, ate it at a dining table without your laptop or phone next to you).

3. Institutional change best happens when you finally get a voice at the decision-making table. Want to know the fastest way to make that happen? Take control of your own destiny. When you decide to invest your energy into growing your career within this professional structure, it puts you in the position to help others coming behind you and creates a healthy and supportive work environment. Start bringing in clients, and the powers to be will take note.

You are at a turning point in your practice; you need to know there is another way that works. Now that you have some serious self-care strategies, it's time to move what's in the way (the chaos in the brain and on the desk) out of the way, to make space for the good stuff.

The Dead-End Game of Blame and Complain

Once upon a time, before the advent of social media, lawyers would grab a drink and the room would quickly ramp up to who could give the most ridiculous story from the week. With no smartphones, we stood around, eating snacks, and allowed ourselves to get all riled up. Then we moved the F—on.

Moving on seems to be a lost art these days. With our world completely connected, our complaints hit volcanic fever within moments, spiraling out of control the minute the juicy details are shared. We are playing a different game now. Pointing fingers and giving it a good shout about is now working against us in an unprecedented fashion.

If you want to attract the perfect clients, and get others to refer you and support you, then you need to stop pointing fingers. (And, let's face it, you need to step away from the constant rhythm of complaining about this great profession you feel has let you down.) Why? First, because bitching is a lousy way to bond. Second, while you're busy ranting, you're undercutting your ability to think, strategize, and problem solve. The goal is to put yourself out there to attract and retain great clients, and that takes being able to see them when they cross your path. When you're in complaining mode, you miss the good stuff, no matter how loud it knocks on your door. With that, let's agree to momentarily set aside the moaning and groaning; instead, change your focus to finding and keeping great clients, who want you to be their trusted advisor for years to come.

To that end, let's play a little game.

Activity:

Set a timer for three minutes. Write down every complaint you have about your work—everything that stinks, every little annoyance, every person who's done you wrong; every single grievance you have against this profession, the practice of law, law school, and your career.

Please consider this your own personal pop-up Festivus. Go!

Awesome. Now, take a deep breath (or three) and set the list to the side.

Let's be clear: This is not about skipping past all the grievances that are sitting in the way of attracting great clients. Nor is it a way for you to point the finger, blame the profession, or get out of doing the work that needs to be done to go find those clients you love to work with and get them to stick around.

Rather, this is the opportunity to place your grievances down on paper—what you would like changed and what is bugging you. You can't fix what you won't admit.

The first step to clearing away the present obstacles that make your day-to-day feel like a bad office sitcom is to acknowledge what isn't working. The key here is to speak to these issues and obstacles with specificity, to make the solutions productive.

Approaches that aren't productive:

1. Posting on social media and hoping your girlfriends from college (and thousands more strangers) jump in and ratify your big complaints with emojis suggesting that the world has become a dumpster fire.

2. Sitting around the campfire at the summer family reunion going on and on about how much your work sucks, as everyone slowly finds another spot on the beach.

3. Complaining in generalities. "You know. It sucks."

4. Offering up the passive aggressive complaint. "It is what it is."

5. Slipping in the pass-it-on complaint. "It was this way for me, now it's time it sucks for you."

6. Obsessing over the silent complaint. Letting it eat you up while you mull it over for hours on end, especially during commute times, and between the hours of 10 p.m. and 2 a.m.

Here is the bad news about all the options above. When you complain in a venting manner, not only do you drive others away (including those great clients you actually enjoy working with), but your brain is not able to process and move on. Rather, the issue is amplified within your own body, marinating in the pit of negativity. Cortisol (the stress hormone) levels increase, which impacts everything from blood sugar, to inflammation in the body, to how you sleep at night. As cortisol levels rise, anxiety ramps up, triggering a host of other issues (yeah . . . increased cortisol has even been shown to slow down metabolism; so, on top of everything else, this sucker can cause potential weight gain and make you feel even lousier). All these things push you deeper into the abyss of misery. The problem is exacerbated by the way we try to solve it.

The Purpose of Venting

Merriam-Webster defines "venting" as the act of giving free expression to a strong emotion. Research shows that when we vent, it creates stronger relationships, allowing us to bond over the misery and common connection to the problem. However, for venting to be effective and healthy, there needs to be a cognitive processing that goes along with the healthy sharing of the problem.[2] This is where we get stuck.

Complaining to everyone (akin to shouting into the wind) is a lot like inviting others to join in our bonfire of complaints, making our problems grow larger rather than being solved. We start filling up our mindset with staggering amounts of negative thoughts that spill over into the rest of our days; they look something like this:

- Your mornings start sluggish. Believing triage is the best way to avoid crisis, you cannot see or identify the priorities for your clients or careers.

- Client interactions are often overlayed with annoyance

---

[2] Check out this article from University of California, Berkely's Greater Good Science Center, which references several excellent studies on venting and its emotional impacts: Jill Suttie, "Does Venting Your Feelings Actually Help?" *Greater Good Magazine*, June 21, 2021, https://greatergood.berkeley.edu/article/item/does_venting_your_feelings_actually_help

or sheer anxiety at the requests and timing of demands, and the need to add one more thing to your insanely long list.

- Networking and anything else non-billable seem extraneous and a waste; your brain suggests you should run before you even begin, since there is no proof it will work.

- Your body is constantly attacked by heartburn, headaches, muscle aches, and a larger host of "body complaints," leaving you to ask how many pain meds you can take.

Imagine the kind of clients who are attracted to those always on edge, angry, and annoyed. Yup, the ones who are going to thrive in that anger and annoyance like a bad virus and cause more grief. Because misery loves company.

At this point, your body and brain may be adversely impacted by the complaining; you may have a host of people angry with you, but still no plan to move forward.

Rather than keep fighting negativity like a bad video game, it's time you find a way to dive into the root cause and use it to transform your daily existence, and years of expertise, into opportunity. Sounds a little like Pollyanna, doesn't it? Yet, this is how we change the negative stress of venting into the positive outcome we desire.

So, how do you make sure your venting is productive and builds bridges with your clients and colleagues? Use moments of frustration to check in with others and see how they are interpreting the situation. If it feels awful to you, it might also for your clients. Hoping everyone ignores the hot issue du jour is missing the opportunity to build a stronger bond. Working with them to move forward is the way to tighten the relationship. When you build stronger bonds with your clients, you keep them coming back for more. The same goes for your colleagues. Magically, they become far more likable. When you build stronger connections with your colleagues, your work life becomes sweeter because they suddenly want to help you when you need it.

The trick is to find ways to bring people together for discussions, rather than inviting everyone to blame-and-complain sessions. Finding a small group that wants to support each other and not get caught in the predicament can do wonders. It can keep you from falling farther into the dark hole and lead to some serious problem solving at the same time.

I stumbled into this years ago when introducing a few colleagues who seemed to be struggling with similar issues. We used a set time to strategize grievances; we've since become an incredible networking and referral group. Now I love to help other lawyers use a similar model and find the support and business development within the small groups that make sense for their practice. Can we call this a win-win-win?

What This Does Not Mean

Back to bitching and moaning, nixing it here and now. Now, this is by no means advocating for abusive clients to always get their way; allowing lackadaisical teams to ignore your pleas for help; or suggesting conflict be avoided at all costs. All these examples are unacceptable and do nothing but harm to the profession. Yet, most of what you want to change lies within your control if you are willing to step aside and test the opportunities.

To see the opportunities for change, to reduce the nonstop noise, and allow time to think and strategize, you must be willing to see the actual problem, understand the available solutions, and be willing to try. That's the key: to try.

Solution: Identify the Crux of Your Complaint

The desire to complain is perfectly understandable. But when your complaints are all wrapped up into some massive lump with no identifiable beginning or end, you need to come at it in another way. Otherwise, you're going to stay in this blame and complain quagmire.

Remember that list of complaints you compiled? Now's the time to use it.

It is intended to guide you toward identifying the core problem—that's the thing you need to address first; it opens space for you to see opportunity and reduces the need to vent willy-nilly. When you identify the underlying issue, you'll be that much better at separating out the stuff that prevents you from seeing the client opportunities worth pursuing.

The thing is the core issue may not be specifically stated on your list.

So, how do you go about finding it when you're locked in the everything-sucks basement—when you have zero time to process? By recognizing you've got a problem and pinpointing what makes you want to complain.

This is the first step to the relief pit stop. And there are two ways to go about it: go to the body or talk it out (with the right person).

First Option: Go to the Body

Most of us feel the problem before we intellectually understand it. Literally. Our bodies process feelings and often react to them far before our brain registers that there is a problem. Legs that ache, a "pit in the stomach," an all-too-often headache register a negative response to a situation that is just begging for our attention. We take ibuprofen hoping the headache goes away, never resolving the underlying issue.

Quashing the symptoms is different than identifying the cause.

Like it or not, to get at the cause—the problem that's keeping you stuck and resistant to take on clients (along with a host of other ways you stay "stuck")—you must head straight into the center of the storm. Instead of being generally fired up at the "man" and the high client demands, you must hyper-focus on the problem. Breathe into it (as the meditation and yoga teachers implore). This allows new energy into the problem; it loosens it, so you can see what it might be. Often this is where you get to explore the root of all blaming and complaining.

To begin, what are you feeling?

1. Frustrated by loose deadlines?

2. Annoyed at constantly changing client specs?

3. Disrespected by a breach of your boundaries?

4. Left out of the good projects?

5. Upset that you seem to never get an invite to the cool kids' table?

Identifying your feelings and the issues catalyzing them (because you stopped long enough to connect with them) leads to possible solutions and a way to circumvent the venting.

1. Frustration leads to a change in how you take on projects and manage the situation up front.

2. Annoyance leads you to embrace that you work with complex clients who want to bring you in for their strategy work, as they are navigating complicated choices during complicated times.

3. Insulted by seeming disrespect leads you to circle back and identify your three to four core values that you can articulate and use as a strength in your practice, rather than using your boundaries to push everything and everyone away.

4. Left out leads to a way to rebuild your community, connections, and relationships in a way that supports where you are now.

The list goes on.

To get to the core of what you want to be doing, who your ideal clients (I like to call them "Ideals") really are, you must tackle this list of grievances one by one. By addressing the core issue and seeing quick results, you can begin moving confidently into a new place. You can begin to fill your practice without losing your bloody mind.

Second Option: Talk It Out, to the Right Person

No, this is not a pitch for business, nor an invitation for you to flood my phone with a list of complaints. Yet, the second option to find the crux of the problem is to find a trusted thinking partner, someone who will listen and help you see and understand the situation from a different vantage point. These are coaches, consultants, or mentors . . . not best friends, members of the PTA, or professional rivals. Blind spots, by definition, are hidden from your view. Having someone step into the story with you—someone who gets it, who has been there and won't get stuck—allows you to go back to working through it the "right" way and resolve it.

Want an example? Let's call her Nell. Nell was sick and tired of clients constantly calling to complain about their worlds, their unresolved problems, and generally sucking up her time, leaving her with stacks of unfinished projects. So, we played out how those conversations started; and within one minute, I asked her to pause. It was clear as day. She started the conversations with a list of ground rules, in a tone that reeked of anger and annoyance. Do you know what that did to the clients? It made them think she wasn't understanding—that within those tight restrictions, she couldn't possibly see their situation. So, they kept talking, thinking they needed to make her understand. But all it did was rile Nell up.

First, we focused on Nell learning to take a deep breath (a real one); to take a deep breath before calls; and to use the calm to streamline and control those client interactions.

Then, we acknowledged the feelings Nell brought to the table (including where she wanted the calls to lead), to craft a new approach to the conversation. Her new plan: move the conversation deliberately; this allows it to progress from the first hello, to the clients being heard and understood, which builds rapport and focuses on efficiency at the same time. No more time suck on Nell's end; no more feelings of being unheard or misunderstood on the clients' end—and Nell feels in control.

This example is a good reminder: the mood you set is contagious to those around you. Clients, colleagues, and friends sense that poop sandwich you are carrying around. They react to the energy, not what you want them to feel. The good news is you can fix this problem by changing your mood and tone, which also influences those around you. And breathing plays a big part. When you learn to stay calm in the storm, it allows others to simmer down, and start to see the problems and options with clarity, rather than chaos.

The Next Step

You must decide you want a positive outcome (and a positive environment to work in).

This may seem obvious, but you would be surprised. Not everyone wants a solution. There is a common battle cry of suffering for associates, new partners, and client demands. Bonding over rants may help you feel seen and understood, while justifying the exhaustion and negative energy that seems to hang around like a dark cloud. Not to mention, complaining (claiming the situation is not fixable) seems to justify walking away from the profession.

But not everyone wants to throw in the towel and give up the law. There is an equally desperate need for another way, for the clouds to break and solutions to appear—for one day that feels easier than the last. To get to that point, you must first be willing to set aside the complaints and the blame, so you can free yourself up to try a few new things.

Activity:

Go back to your list of grievances. Read through it. Circle the issues that need your attention. Star the most critical. Strike out those that are either combined in another, or not your issue to resolve. Do you know how to recognize the ones that are not yours to resolve and are you willing to step away from those at this point? Something to consider.

For all the "starred" issues, take one minute, and brainstorm all the other ways to look at the issue. (If you have a laundry list of said issues, do yourself a favor and pick two.) Do you see a solution? Are there conversations worth having? What are you curious about—what is worth putting oxygen into the problem, working through it, and seeing the opportunities to grow through them, rather than staying stuck in the cycle of blame and complain?

Example: Let's say the problem is that clients are always flaming angry at you for falling behind, yet they never get you the information you need to complete the work, which causes crazy amounts of anxiety. What are other ways to view this issue?

1. Clients are stuck running through an internal process that could use some help in simplifying approvals.

2. The clients don't understand what you need to do after you get the information.

3. Deadlines haven't been discussed with the clarity or severity necessary to calm everyone down.

4. The problems and issues need to be broken down to a simpler way of working through them.

5. The client is on vacation.

6. The business unit is on vacation.

7. Someone got sick (um, a pandemic).

8. The personal life of client is in upheaval. (They have parents, kids, and spouses just like the rest of us.)

One more thing. Can you think of a time you managed the situation rather than just pushed it aside? Pick out at least one of these moments in your past and mark it down on the timeline. This is part of what you bring to your practice and the expertise you innately share with clients.

Similarly, is there a time when you remained calm in the storm? Turns out this is a power move. When you can control your breath and be the calm one in the room, you start to lead the conversation rather than follow the chaos.[3]

---

[3] I have a few easy breathing exercises to practice, way before you are in the hot seat and tempers are flying. Check them out in the Guide. debfeder.com/guide.

Ditch the Daily Scramble

Have you experienced that moment where you recognized something had to change? For me, it was around 11 p.m., *West Wing* murmuring in the background, my bed covered with papers. I was trying to catch up with the day. Exhausted, I wondered why in the world this had become the time I got the real work done, after triaging for everyone else since dawn. That's when I knew things had to change. In a flash, my years of in-house experience (and memories) collided with my private practice. I knew without a doubt the practice of law could be different; not only was I all in for this change, but I also wanted to lead the charge toward a solution.

At 8 a.m. the next morning, I started knocking on partner doors and picking up the phone to talk to colleagues and clients. I put out the craziest bold promise:

> *Let me train the clients' corporate teams, and we can save time, money, and frustration. Let me coach the attorneys and offer up the programs we need (which back then sounded like time management and practice planning),*

> *and we will start to see results for everyone involved. Let me make it easier, more efficient, and truthfully cost-effective for the clients, while building their trust and getting more work. Let me collaborate with the lawyers to be better for our clients.*

Call it kismet, call it what you want, but the stars aligned, and my clients and the partners in charge were willing to follow my lead.

But that 11 p.m. wake-up call is known as the daily scramble. There is nothing that keeps you away from finding and nurturing great clients like the constant scramble you call a career. If you are serious about building up your practice, filled with clients you love (and who love you) then you must be willing to work and manage your days in a new way.

Why, you ask?

1. Working in circles is a fast way to get nowhere.

2. While you're busy with your head down, answering emails and focusing on being quick to reply, someone else is talking to the people you dream of working with, and building the relationships you need to be seeking out.

The goal is to manage your days in a way that allows you to engage with great clients and be their thinking partner. You should be the one they reach out to first when big (and small) problems land in their laps. Stop spinning in circles and leave the morning scramble for the eggs (that you finally have time to eat with your family before heading out the door).

Now, for some data . . .

Two Quick Questions:

1. On a scale of 1 to 5 (1 being "my life feels like a spa day;" 5, "my hair is on fire"), how do you feel about your average day-to-day workload?

2. How many emails are in your inbox right now (read and unread)?

If you're like many, you rise before the sun; you may snag a cup of coffee, workout, shower; pack lunches, clean up the house. You swipe through the first emails of the day to identify impending crises; you somehow find a way to throw on clothes and head to the office or launch into the virtual space.

The day quickly moves into triage mode, knocking off emails like a bad game of whack-a-mole.

You're not alone. Most wake to find hundreds of early morning notes and questions piled up in their inbox. In 2015, alone, the average attorney managed 17,000 emails per year.[4] With enhanced technology and messaging options, I'm willing to say that number has most certainly skyrocketed.

What do each of these emails, texts, and instant messages need? A reply. And time is of the essence because delayed responses (even if momentarily delayed) cause you to spiral into the worry of being ghosted.

A world that banked on the premise of thoughtful analysis has turned into a lesson in efficient reactions. You answer so many questions—spend an exorbitant amount of time trying to prioritize and manage—that you cannot answer the simplest of questions at the end of the day.

Our connection to our devices, to the endless email stream, has pulled us even further away from our connection to colleagues, friends, and family—even ourselves. We're all guilty: sitting there, staring at a device right in front of clients, barely paying attention to the conversation in the room because we feel responsible to keep everything moving.

---

[4] "Surprising Statistics about Lawyer Information Overload," *Metajure: Work Smarter*, April 25, 2016, https://metajure.com/surprising-statistics-lawyer-information-overload/.

Which puts you in a quandary. How do you balance the chaos of the day and allow technology to be the support and solution, rather than part of the challenge; how do you let it serve, not destroy, you?

Before we talk about your inbox, and how to manage it, let's deal with something bigger: the general sense of chaos.

Control the Constant Chaos

Living the life you want, begins with control of your days . . . starting with first thing in the morning. Though it may be helpful for some, we're not talking the rigid formality hyped on social media for successful people, here (hit the gym, drink a liter of filtered warm water with a slice of lemon and cucumber, and meditate in pure silence).

Rather, it's the fact that allowing your days to be managed by the chaos of others is a choice. This chaos lives primarily in your inbox and in the reactionary mode of others who use the "loudest wins" strategy to move their priorities up on your list. Changing this dynamic is hard because everyone needs something more important than putting yourself on the priority list (or so it seems). Basically, it's a reward for martyring yourself on the altar of hustle and grind.

Sure, the old-school mentality of scramble and hustle may seem the road to success, but if you put that aside, you'll find you can show up even more responsive, impressive, and awesome. And when you do, you'll wow the kind of clients that will make your career start to look like that fantasy you envisioned years ago.

The State of the Problem

The idea of stepping out of the madness may leave you paralyzed with fear. After all, the influx of emails, project levels, and client expectations has many racing from dawn to dawn (yeah, you read that right). The excuses are all the same: "You don't understand, clients won't tolerate a delay"; "our practice is different than others"; "our billable rates require us to see those emails and respond within seconds."

The list goes on. But this is not advocating for ignoring crises, nor suggesting you tell clients and partners to sit down and relax. There is a more efficient way to get the real work done, build your book of business, and answer those emails.

But before the solutions, here's a look at what your inbox cannot be:

1. An endless task list. Expecting yourself to weed through the masses of emails and remember that one thing to get done is possibly the most inefficient thing you can do each day.

2. Your own personal video game. You're not playing beat

the clock trying to see how fast you can respond to an email as it barely lands in the box. This quick-fire reaction often is the one that causes a whole lot more grief in the long run.

3. A filing cabinet. Leaving all your emails in the inbox, just in case you need them one day, is not organization, nor is it a form of productivity.

4. Your CYA file. Certain that clients might come back one day and try to point the finger at everyone and everything, you want to make sure you save everything just in case. That's great. There's a place for that. It's called the file room. Not your inbox.

Here's a novel approach to technology, productivity, and an egregious inbox:

Sticky notes. And a timer. (Trust me, I'll explain later, but first . . .)

In all seriousness, how do you deal with the chaos? How do you eliminate nonsense in your inbox?

1. Stop disrespecting the inbox of other people.

In other words, think before you send. Do you need to copy everyone in the firm on an email about the department meeting running too long? Better yet, do you need to send the note at all? As attorneys, our paranoid level of covering our asses and micromanaging has become so advanced that we document everything and anything, often leaving everyone else scratching their heads and ignoring half of what we send them. Stop contributing to the white noise.

Use alternate forms of communication; oftentimes, it will surprise and delight your clients and colleagues. The most helpful and most underused? The telephone. Knowing how, and when, to pick up the phone and talk something over with a client or colleague is a skill. Even more so, leaving the effective voicemail that will get returned. We are so used to the barrage of emails, and forced video meetings, that allowing ourselves to use the old-fashioned telephone simply amazes many clients.

Not to mention, a phone call (talking through the problem) is just easier. When you exchange emails, half the contents get lost in translation, due to over-zealous ramblings intended to fill the background information like a dirty kitchen sink.

Imagine, having a client answer the phone and getting the whole thing settled in a matter of minutes. No more scrambling and hoping you aren't being ghosted (by either party). Pick up the phone and give it a try.

2. Make a list that works instead of using your inbox (or legal pad).

Lawyers love their legal pads, page after page, just waiting to be filled. But here's where the sticky notes come in. There's only so much you can write on a three-inch square piece of paper. If it doesn't fit, you don't write it. This is how you simplify your list and focus on a couple of priorities; this allows your brain to wrap around those tasks, rather than splitting time and energy muddling through countless entries in a legal pad, trying to distill down to the next thing to do among way too many options.

There is a whole lot of science backing up the inefficiency of multitasking, but for now, know that it's a time suck and your brain isn't as good at it as you want to believe. But I digress . . .

Back to the sticky notes. You have one note for each day; complete what's on it. As you do, it will build the momentum you need to prioritize, shift the long list clogging your brain into action items, and roll right into the next priority.

But to know what to write on that sticky note, you need to separate what's important from the noise. To get the ball rolling, pick a task from your inbox that will take about thirty minutes to complete; jot it down on a little piece of paper, and get it done.

3. Crunch time.

Think about it; how often have you started the weekend wanting to clean the house, only to get to Sunday night, wondering where the time went (and why your house remains messy) or you set goals for the year, but you're barely able to remember what they were, come December? Happens all the time.

It's time to work like my in-laws just announced they're in town and coming over for dinner. Because when that happens, I can clean the entire house, set the table, and cook a (good) meal in less than twenty minutes.

So, how do you make this happen? Shorten the time needed to get things done. Break down priorities into manageable tasks. Hunting down those quick tasks first helps get the ball rolling. Once you conquer the small task, it rolls into the next one. You're crunching time. When you keep tasks to five or ten minutes, rather than waiting for full days without interruption, you quickly gain control of how your days unfold and what you are actually getting done.

4. Play the cleanup game.

Do you remember cleanup time in preschool? Well, those teachers were on to something. "Clean up; clean up; everybody, clean up!" Let this be your rallying cry to start controlling your inbox. Set your timer for five minutes and go! Sort. File. Delete.

Don't stop; this is not the time for lengthy replies, nor is it the time to keep piling up in there. This is all about the clean.

First, sort by "subject." This will quickly show you how a string of 55 emails lead to one. File the one; delete the other 54.

Some other time during the week, set your timer for five minutes more, and sort your inbox by "name." This quickly shows you the list serves and subscriptions you have been getting for that one coupon you needed two years ago, which has resulted in 500 emails just sitting in your inbox.

Another option is to start the cleanup party at the bottom of your inbox. That poor, oldest email is collecting dust like nobody's business. Go get it and figure out if it still needs a spot on center court.

This game, or email triage, should be done frequently, but only in five-minute chunks.

5. Pick and choose what you listen to.

You need to intentionally pay close attention to the voices you allow to manage your days and guide your goals. When you are scrambling, you instinctively respond to the loudest voices, the fastest emails, the brightest ding in your technology-filled universe. Your fight-flight response senses danger in the anger and urgency. Calming this down will allow you to carefully evaluate the priorities using your actual knowledge and experience.

As you change the time and focus, you can start paying attention to what you have been hired to do: provide big thoughts on complicated matters. Getting beyond the noise is necessary to allow your expertise to make it to the table. This means you've got to pace yourself; find the stride that works for and with your own practice and business endeavors. Find the solution that balances not just what you want, but what your clients need as well. This includes having the insight to know which voices to pay attention to, in which moments.

6. Decide what gets in and what stays out.

Some people call these boundaries. But this overused, and often misunderstood phrase, can be interpreted as telling everyone "No." While "no" certainly has its place, just a blanket statement for anything that feels uncomfortable, can often have far-reaching consequences— including seriously missed opportunities, and more chaos than necessary.

It is critical that this step gets broken down the right way. Think of it as setting up the foundation of your home. The taller or wider you want a house, the stronger you need to set the foundation. That foundation anchors four walls—with one value (or boundary) for each. Not everything can make its way into the foundation, only the important stuff. Also, it's important to know that as your career and life change, so do your values and foundational strengths.[5]

7. Communicate those boundaries without killing the relationship.

There is a lot of chatter that boundaries help manage your day, but it is knowing how to communicate the real ones effectively that makes the difference. That's the power of a boundary. It's not just saying you have one; it is certainly not setting rules for your practice and answering everyone and everything with a hard "no."[6] Once you get to this advanced step, you can use these boundaries as an incredible conversation starter, content builder, and client generation tool.

Here's an example from my own experience. I used to work with a partner who always cut people down. (I now know this was a defense mechanism, but at the time it drove me bananas.) While we were often partnered together on projects, every time

---

[5] This Guide exercise is critical to complete. Knowing what values make up your foundation right now (and how to identify them as they change) sets the stage for knowing exactly what work to start bringing your way. This allows you to change the way you work, to make sure it fits for you and your boundaries.

[6] There are certainly times for a hard "no." (Do I need to make a list for you? Anything unethical, illegal, or just plain wrong falls into this category.) It's just not intended for whenever the inconvenient rush project comes along.

I left his office, I felt kind of sick to my stomach. The harsh way he cut at others was too much.

Until that point, I didn't think it mattered if the people I worked with were kind; I didn't stand around waiting for hugs and smiles all the time. A self-prescribed badass, I could handle the toughest of situations. But I could not ignore that pit in my stomach every time I finished a conversation. It was a clear response to the environment. Instead of ignoring it, I hyper-focused into it. (Remember when we talked about going into the body and paying attention? This is an example of how that works.) After quick reflection, I decided I needed to focus my work on being with people who spoke about others (and to me) with kindness. Since I couldn't stop working with him, I moved our communication to email or the phone, and my world became a much happier and more productive place.

The Truth

Chaos is a choice. You will continue to scramble until you decide to put some small actions into place to change the way you approach your days: make your inbox work with and for you, not something you are trying to beat; crunch time; clean up the mess; pick the voices you listen to, and set a firm foundation based on communicating your legit boundaries.

Once this happens, you are ready to move past the trouble you've gotten yourself into and start building the career you want, filled with the great clients you know are waiting for you.

Activity:

Someone suggested this game to me when I returned from maternity leave, and I have since shared it with thousands of professionals. As covered in this chapter, you must beat the numbers. But before I give you the plan, grab one more sticky note. Write down the total number of emails currently in your inbox (all of them, not just unread—I know how you think). Once you have that number, email it to deb@debfeder.com and ask for the email game. I will send it right over. Seriously, it puts this all together and makes it a game you want to win.

When you finally decide to change your days, you have taken a ginormous step toward the middle of that rope you're clinging to. Your grip becomes a little firmer; you start to let go of that feeling that your world might fall apart in a moment. Congrats! With this new foundation, you are going to take another big step forward as you embrace opportunity and what's next.

Be Brave

When I was in the third grade, we took swimming lessons. No joke, in Cedar Rapids, Iowa, they bused the entire grade, every week, to some pool where we were forced to take swim lessons, complete with a final jump off the platform diving board. Not just the low board, but the high dive. Seriously, it was worthy of an Olympian. And we didn't pass this nightmare of a swimming class until we had tackled that feat.

When I'm worried about trying something new, I think of that jump. If I did that, surely, I can tackle those big daunting goals that seem out of reach. It can apply to you, too. If only you begin to think about bravery every day, with your own career, like those little kids lined up, ready to climb a towering ladder . . . and jump. Because it's the stuff that scares the poo out of us that's worth getting on that ladder. So, ask yourself, what it would look like to take 5 percent of that bravery and infuse it into your plans to go get those clients. My vote—get climbing and enjoy the view before you take the plunge. You build confidence by becoming brave. Particularly when looking for the perfect client.

The perfect-client fantasy turns out to be flawed. Because even if you meet the perfect client, you aren't done. In fact, you have picked a profession that is never finished meeting people. Instead, it's a revolving door of deals, projects, questions, and people, all needing something from you. The whole thing is built off interpersonal relationships: building them, nurturing them, understanding them, and responding to them. No matter your years of practice or niche of expertise, you are in the relationship game. To get that desired book of business, you need to summon your courage and start playing it—in a way that works for you.

While some call this cycle of meeting people "networking," that tends to smack the scary sticker on it. Instead, think of the secret to building relationships something akin to that ladder leading up to the diving board: you simply take it one step at a time.

Meet someone. Build a smidge of rapport. Get to know that person. Take in the new view. Then build the relationship. Engage in the next conversation. Understand the next issue. Be open to the next relationship and conversation along the way.

What Typically Happens

You meet someone at an event or meeting, exchange cards (or promise to connect on LinkedIn), and bring the card back to the desk. After staring at it for a week or two, you plop it into the recycle bin, thinking it has been too long. *They won't remember you. It would be foolish to follow up now.* Yet during that time, you thought about it, over and over again, just not sure what to say. *Would they want to hear from you? What can you offer them? You don't want to be weird. Maybe that initial conversation wasn't all that awesome. They probably already have an attorney they love.*

Sure, they asked you to follow up, but they were probably being nice. And anyway, it's been too long now. So, never mind. Maybe next time.

Do you see what just happened? You chose to opt out of the game before it ever started. Why? You're afraid of rejection, plain and simple.

Truth: There is a zero percent chance of getting any traction in business development if you don't try.

Truth: Trying often requires more than one touch point.

Truth: The bravery required each step of the way is enough to make you puke.

Truth: Building your book of business won't be easy, but it can be simple.

Truth: It can work. And you will live.

Truth: You've got to treat it like a skill that's learned.

To change this story, you must go back and remember when you weren't afraid of everything going wrong.

When you were a kid, you tried new things. Back then it was fun, not risky. Falling on the ski slopes? Bounce back up and race to the finish line. Riding a bike? A few skinned knees weren't going to keep you out of the neighborhood fun. The list goes on and on: cooking, art, trying out for cheerleading—or, my personal favorite, synchronized swimming (oh yes, I did).

But once your career got a little movement, things began to change. Your head was down; you began to feel constant worry over one thing: not screwing up. You stopped practicing bravery for yourself and moved into protective mode. The stakes got a little bigger. The opportunities to stretch your "do something new" muscles got used less and less. And the path to falling became more imminent and more severe.

Maybe it's mortgage payments, the fear of being cut out of the next project, or having to put that resume together again, but you stopped stepping out of line. You focused on what you're good at and stayed in the safe zone. This immediate fear of failure (or looking stupid) coupled with a career that is wrapped in risk-adversity creates the perfect storm. One that you must grapple with when it comes to expanding your practice so you can put yourself out there for your clients.

Activity:

Make a quick list of every time you can remember taking a risk by trying something new. Once you are done, look at the list and rate each instance.

Rate it 1 to 5 (1 being easy-peasy; 5, hard as hell). Then rate it (1, a waste of time; 5, totally worth it).

What do you notice?

For example, you took risks applying to schools and going for the jobs. You answered the tough questions in front of classmates and put your name on the list for on-campus interviews. You were still brave. When things didn't go your way, you hired tutors or took the prep class. (Maybe the firm paid for high-end bar review classes to make sure you were ready or you found a study group.)

Notice a theme? When the stakes seemed to rise, you got help. You found your people to help you out. You came to the game, prepared by the experts.

In other words, you layered the high-end support with community. In fact, research on networks and support for those rising in their careers is clear: those who do it well, have their tight networks of people backing them up, supporting them, introducing them, and cheering them on.[7]

The Love/Hate Relationship with Risk

An attorney, by nature, is put in the position to measure, hyper-analyze, and take care of risk decisions for clients. You put yourself, your humility, and your worth on the line, assuming you are being judged on whether they pick you for the next project or next pitch.

The story you have told yourself is even thinking of being successful requires an obscene amount of risk. With so many "what ifs" on the line, it won't pan out; you'll never live it down. So, it's better to stand back until you are ready, until you're willing to step bravely into the unknown.

So, what can you do? Well, you need to be willing to take the chance—to not know whether it will work—to put yourself out there and be willing to learn how to do this stuff. That's how you build confidence.

When it comes to client development, what's the worst that could happen?

---

[7] Brian Uzzi, "Research: Men and Women Need Different Kinds of Networks to Succeed," *Harvard Business Review*, February 25, 2019, https://hbr.org/2019/02/research-men-and-women-need-different-kinds-of-networks-to-succeed.

1. You get ghosted.
2. They say, "Not now."
3. They say, "No thanks."
4. You botch the conversation.
5. You botch the work.
6. They don't like you.
7. You don't like them.
8. You end up hating the work.
9. They don't hire you.
10. They do hire you and it doesn't go well.
11. They do hire you and it goes too well.

My theory: we are most afraid of the first and last items on this list.

Fear #1: Being Ignored

Ghosting. The non-response; this is where it's easy to get bogged down. You assume they got the note and are standing around with a group of colleagues, laughing at you. They're ignoring you because they don't know how to tell you they aren't interested in the conversation.

Somewhere along the lines, our society normalized the idea of ghosting as an acceptable response. It's being disliked at the deepest level. And it makes you so good at layering assumptions when you don't hear back that you don't consider what else could be going on.

Here are a few other options:

- Remember how your inbox is full? Same for your clients.
- Remember how you often forget to call someone back by the end of the day? Same for your clients.
- Remember how you are nervous to pick up the phone, and want someone else to do the organizing? Same for your clients.
- Remember how you are balancing competing opinions and hate difficult conversations? Same for your clients.

The lesson: get objective rather than making assumptions about what happened to your email request for a conversation. Instead of working yourself up over the fact that you haven't heard back, change your email strategy, and make sure you are progressing the conversation to elicit the best chance of a response, and future conversation.

Fear #2: It Works

Now, fear of being ignored is one thing, but you may be even more afraid of it all working out. Because what happens when you not only get a response but business out of it? Success is enough to scare the living crap out of you.

You spend so much time worrying and filling yourself with fear of everything falling apart, you forget to prepare yourself for success. You talk in generalities. You imagine making partner. Equity partnership is the real goal, but you wouldn't dare speak of it for fear that it could happen. While the devil is in the details, you keep your big dreams at bay by focusing on the one million ways it could all go wrong. You are scared the whole thing could work out. Then what will you do?

The fear of success is so great, it often leads to incredible mental scenarios that keep the good stuff locked away. *If someone responds to your client development efforts:*

1. They will give you too much work to manage.

2. You don't have a good enough team to impress them.

3. You've never worked for a client that great before, so it's probably a mistake.

4. The other firm is a better fit for them.

5. You haven't handled that exact kind of project before; it would take too much to start now.

6. It might make your career explode, and your life disappear.

Stuck in this quandary, you stay still. You don't reach out; you don't engage in conversations; you don't send an email to which they can reply. You hope there will be a sign telling you what to do; better yet, you hope the perfect client lands on your plate, without having to take the risk one way or the other. Standing in the center of this great balancing act, you wait for the universe to wave its magic wand.

Then, you do what any self-respecting lawyer knows how to do when faced with the fear of success: you micromanage (your inbox, conversations, documents—what everyone is wearing in the room). Since success is not something you can put on the checklist, you try to hyper-control every little detail, allowing you some semblance of control over your practice, life, and the stuff sitting on your plate.

But do you know what happens when you try to control something? You're so hard on it, it breaks. The same goes for your practice and success. You need to learn to guide the clients and your career so you don't end up breaking everything with your incessant micromanaging.

To get in the habit of guiding your career, put yourself out there—fail a bit; recognize that it will not destroy you—then try again.

Said another way:

1. Decide to try.
2. Try it.
3. Reflect: what works, what doesn't.
4. Learn fast.
5. Be brave and try again.

The Not-So-Good Alternative

In our quest for protecting ourselves, our income, our reputation, we often jump at the chance for any client. It seems like the safe choice, since we are not leaving good money or hours on the table for someone else. Knowing instinctively that it is not a right decision, we still opt-in for safety and control of something rather than nothing. I have done this; and I am willing to bet that you have, too.

Or you play it small.

Not to be confused with picking safety, playing small is a defense mechanism against those big audacious goals that may involve someone mocking you or exposing you as a fraud. Since you never want to be considered braggadocio, you shrink your goals, and play inside the box you think everyone expects you to hang out in. Talk about a confidence killer.

While you are stepping into your big, brave goals, you must have an honest conversation with yourself about what matters. Not in the traditional sense (money, title, career path), but what serves you and can lead to your big goals. This is not an invitation to throw caution to the wind, not give a damn, and start burning bridges. It's an invitation to tap into your wisdom—to learn about what you want to build in your career, and why, before moving forward. To be brave enough to move forward.

To have a desk full of clients you love, you are going to have to let go and allow them to find you. And it all starts with this exercise.

Activity:

Take three minutes and put down on paper every idea, plan, or goal that comes to mind when you think about expanding your career, building a book, and bringing in new clients. It doesn't matter how silly, random, or specific. Just write. After three minutes, step back and reread what you wrote.

Go back through and circle the words and phrases that jump out at you. Which ones seem the easiest? Which feel the most aligned with your vision for the "great-big-perfect-practice" you are working to build? What is one thing you can do to move it forward today, in ten minutes? Do that one thing to get it moving.

Why? Because round things roll. When we put our plan in motion, even just a smidge, things will naturally start to move forward. Just give it a nudge and see what happens.

Confidently Own Your Spot at the Table

I will never forget the first time I spent a holiday with my husband's family. We walked in and were seated at the kids' table. All the other tables were filled with grown-ups, complete with nice linens and real coffee cups . . . and there we were at the back of the family room, seated before a disposable tablecloth and a plastic coffee cup. I was about thirty years old.

But you see, my husband was not just the oldest child in his family, he was the oldest cousin. There was no one even close to our age. He was considered a kid. So, I was, too. I spent this meal in awe of the fourteen-year-old at the table relaying his antics from the night before at the school dance. In all fairness, I am not sure anyone else was even twenty at this point. Dating to them meant the prom, or maybe a sorority barn dance. And here we were, about to move in together, talking refrigerators and mortgages, and picking out a wedding date around the corner. We needed to move up from the kids' table.

To start building your book, and take control of your practice, you must decide to pick up your plate, tell someone to scootch over, and find a spot for yourself at the power table. Owning your space and place with the big kids (or dare I say, the adults), will help get the ball rolling. Namely, a new attitude and respect for you and your practice will start rolling your way. Let's be clear: the new attitude must start with you. Waiting for someone else to treat you differently is a waste of time, and a lesson in madness.

Being seated at the kids' table is only part of the story. You may be telling yourself that it could be taken away in a moment. That you probably don't want it. Or they don't want you. They want shinier, smarter, better, older, stronger, meaner . . . you get the picture.

The flaws in this thinking are many. It is a combination of a lousy structure that has been cemented in the law firm model and tradition for decades, and your own lousy mindset. That means getting away from the kids' table does not happen with a change of title, but a change of approach.

Optimally, the momentum toward partnership would put your head right; yet too often, it's a surprise when you look around and realize you are still being treated like a higher-paid associate. This wake-up call jump-starts some sort of action that looks like a scramble to hunt down clients, network, and put yourself out there. Often with mediocre results because let's face it, you haven't necessarily done this before. As it turns out, the path to that power position isn't happening if you play the martyr and keep acting like the cranky teen who hasn't gotten their way in the room.

People often behave and respond to those around them in a way they are used to. What does this look like in a law firm? Partners like the reliable attorney to stay the reliable attorney. They like to be the person in charge, the one clients depend on, and if we're being honest, the one getting the credit at the end of the year for the hard work and care of this client relationship. When you move up, or dare I say, want more, it rocks the boat.

Regardless of firm structure, getting the clients you want starts with you and your mindset. I know I'm repeating myself, but let's face it, you've got to hear this message above the noise. Your mindset must catch up with your expertise and experience, be you a partner or not. That means getting real about what you've done, how you got here, and the micro-moments that add up to make you the incredible attorney you are today.

Activity:

Grab that timeline you started putting together.

Look at the years and positions you have held since you started practicing law. Start adding the lessons you have learned, the positions you had on teams, deals, or cases. When did clients start calling you? Do you remember the first note you received complimenting the outcome; your first time in court; or the first time the deal was your responsibility? These are all little steps away from being considered the little kid in the room. Because little kids, they don't get the big clients.

Next, take note of when you developed a bit of expertise: a new perspective on, or approach to, your work; when someone junior to you started showing up on projects; when you were suddenly giving directions more often than receiving them.

Depending on where you are in your practice, you must start noticing how it has evolved, and how you have, too. Confidently owning your presence in your practice is a big step toward getting away from everyone looking at you for low-level work.

Now that the timeline is getting a little crowded, let's give it a little happy dance.[8] *You have done so much to get to this point. No one will recognize it quite the way you do. And no one else actually matters at the end of the day. Crank on the tunes . . . and dance!*

[8] Did you put this on your Guide timeline? debfeder.com/guide.

Look Up

Once you get comfortable that you are not meant to stay in the corner taking notes, you will realize that the clients call you, want your perspective, and are looking at you to quarterback the whole deal. It has probably already happened, but you were so busy with your head down, you didn't even notice. Well, look up!

That's the next step: look up, look around, and take notice of what is going on around you.

Start taking notes on what you observe about each deal (or case). What are you working on? Are you included in the client conversations? Who else is a part of the team? Pay attention. Ask questions. Get involved and engaged wherever and whenever possible. Waiting for the formal invite to arrive in the mail is a waste of time and is never going to happen. Making yourself indispensable to the clients and their end goals gets you a spot saved at the table. Be the curious one who cares. Because that's what gets them to call you.

Years ago, I helped close a deal around the holidays. There was only one person left at the company who needed to be around for the closing, and way too many of her friends had been let go as part of the transaction. She called me, crying. She knew I was waiting for that last fax (yeah, that tells you how long ago it was). She couldn't get the fax machine to work and was at the end of her tether. Want to know what I did? I told her to grab tissues and relax. I talked to her about her memories with her team. While in the background, I was furiously sending messages to every tech member of my office that could help triage this with me. I didn't tell her to deal. I didn't ignore the pain. I found the solution, while being human. Getting curious about someone and their work and allowing them the space to be human is the combination that makes for a solid client relationship. So, do more than simply get the deal across the finish line. Be human. That's worth so much.

Own Your Own Practice

The turning point is when you decide to have a grown-up private law practice. It starts by owning some decisions about it. Not just "give me the career of my dreams," but the bigger questions that give you answers to how best to step away from being the junior in the room.

Pay attention to the following:

1. How have you hit a homerun for clients?
2. Which conversations do you enjoy?
3. When do you do your best work?
4. Why are you energized by certain projects, people, and

opportunities, and not by others?

5. Who could you hang out with all day, and who needs to step aside?

6. Where have you caught glimpses of your book of business evolving in the future?

Taking a practice apart and looking at it from many different angles allows you to start picking the simplest changes. The answers will often become super clear, super fast. Because you are now sitting at the exact point when deciding to act like a grown-up can have a life-altering impact on the practice of your dreams.

Even with this plan to practice with a new self-respect, you cannot ignore the fact that the decision to change your space and place is not entirely up to you. So, how do you get unstuck from this spot? Carefully.

Stop Looking for a Way Out

Do you know what I remember of my mother's funeral? OK, there are quite a few things, but one in particular is a tour bus that had road-tripped from office to office, picking up employees, clients, and colleagues. They spilled out of my house, eager to share the stories—to cry, and laugh, and lecture me as they had done since I was eight years old and wanted to answer the office phones.

These people were committed to my parents because my parents were committed to them. While I loved these people, whenever anyone asked if I was going "into the business," this wasn't an option my parents put on the table. Had they done so, I would have used it as a way out of finding my own way. You see, my parents could see further for me than I could see for myself. My life was not meant to be following them, or anyone for that matter.

This sage advice works in developing a practice, too. You need to recognize and allow yourself to see further than where you are right now. Of course, there are many ways to try and get around doing the stuff needed for the interest of getting and keeping clients.

For one, there is an old school idea that you join the firm, do solid work, get in good with the senior partner and the partner's clients, and wait. Wait until the senior partner decides it's time to finally step away from the desk, take that trip around the world, and set sail on the next adventure (also known as retirement).

This is a terrible "own your own book" strategy because:

1. It assumes you like the partner and the partner's clients, and the clients like you, with limited effort. If you have read this far, you have hopefully started to realize that while expertise and experience play into our client development, the relationships are built from authentic conversations, which are a match of personality and approach. Likeability is just a factor hanging over it like a big umbrella. It will feel like you are stuck out in the rain when it doesn't fit.

2. It also assumes no one else is vying for this book and going to grab it from underneath you. If you think you are the only one seeing the numbers and stars aligning, you probably haven't looked up from your desk lately. Nothing sucks worse than finding out that the senior partner and clients have been strategizing this for years, and someone else has been tapped as team lead, with you continuing a stellar supporting role.

3. If you take the clients, you get their problems, too. Over time we train our clients on what to expect from us. If you take the senior partner's clients, they are going to expect that you follow the same rules that they have gotten used to over the years. The good comes with the baggage. While not complicated to comprehend, it is incredibly complicated to overcome and change. Clients get trained and carry with them expectations of approach and service levels. If they have been the senior partner's bread and butter, they assume you will have the same approach and gravitas they have come to expect from the guy who liked to wine and dine them at the club, and take long afternoons filled with drinks and golf, all while listening to their complaints and writing down their bills for the friend.

4. Clients often look for someone new in times of transition. Shifts allow for openings. When you move one piece, the next opening seems to pop up quickly. Maybe the client never realized how annoyed they were with your billing systems, or just put up with the long-distance relationship for old-time's sake. With the exit, they see opportunity to craft it the way they have always imagined it could be. Another common occurrence here is the in-house counsel that has always wanted to select their own firms finally have an opening to make a new introduction and build the team of support that they want. Or bring the work in-house. Not what they inherited.

5. Clients aren't sticking with the same firm anymore. Times have changed. This started to shift a couple decades back, but the dinosaur pace of change with institutional clients and law firms has this still evolving. Still, the impacts are noticed much more often now. Firms are constantly scrambling for the attention and business from clients. The savvy ones are following a lot of the advice found in this book and nurturing the relationships from the wings . . . and waiting. You have no idea they are there; the stealth moves are well rehearsed, and the innovative solutions and better response times are just waiting to take the work as the senior partner exits through the wings.

6. Other factors. This one is vague enough to give you a burst of confidence, until you realize you aren't considered part of the strategy. This is when the in-house team wants to realign the strategy with firm support. They might be looking for a different angle for team lead (moving from a litigator to corporate counsel); they might want diverse views at the table; to blend different firms; or to bring the expertise in-house altogether.

There is one more significant problem with using the waiting game to magically build your book: you must buy into this-approach and be willing to practice patience for a hope and a prayer. If I only had a nickel for every big law attorney who told me they wouldn't need to know how to do business development because their clients are "institutional," I would be bathing in money. Because these are the same attorneys who circle back and realize that it was a big fat lie they told themselves.

The Definition of Business Development

Let's remind ourselves what business development is at the core: clients (and colleagues) picking you for the project team; clients calling you with the questions (big and small); clients and referral partners throwing out your name when asked who will be the go-to for answers. I don't care if the client has worked with the firm for generations, that is a game of the past (as we have already discussed above). You are still just one body in a sea of attorneys, and you need to be picked to be at the table.

The Choices

By now it should be clear that you are going to have to make some changes. It's not about running away or taking a blind leap. But if you're thinking you must first consider all the options, here's a good start; the real strategy and path tends to be a blend—making changes from different angles, in a way that works for your practice and big plans.

Some of the options:

1. Start walking. Decide whether you want to walk out the door or quit following the path that everyone has set out for you. This choice has you finding a new space and new

clients that want to treat you with the respect you deserve. While this option is always on the table (depending on the current job market and your circumstances), it comes with a whole different set of issues to grapple with. Is a new place or plan any different than what you are walking away from? What will you gain? What are you leaving behind?

2. Change the view from the inside. This plan has you remaining in your same position but moving the pieces and conversations such that you are no longer looked down upon or relied on for the junior position. (This might be leading the team or sharing in the origination for your part of the relationship.) You want to keep working hard, scrambling all day, hoping one day the respect will come internally with the title, and opportunities commiserate with the experience and investment the firm has put into your training and practice. This is an option. It will take conversations. Possibly some difficult ones. But, often worth it.

   Of course, you don't walk into these conversations unprepared and ready for battle. It's critical you take the time to prep your case, lay the groundwork with members of the team, and know who is going to have your back in these discussions.

3. Build the book, and the respect will come. When you decide to own your expertise and experience before anyone else rubber stamps it, and you use this as a confident start to

conversations and working with clients, you change the game, and let the firm catch up to you. Bringing in business and putting yourself in the leadership position (doesn't matter what the firm wants to call you because leadership is not a title), you allow yourself the control and power over your practice. You get to set the pace and the path. Once this happens, where and with whom you are meant to practice becomes a whole lot clearer.

4. Walk in and demand to be considered the heir apparent. This never goes all that well; it ruffles feathers and pretty much guarantees the client and partners are ready for you to move on and find new teams to work with. Not recommended.

5. Build a coalition. Making things happen is so much better when you work with others, rather than just trying to grab your piece of the pie. Bring together those who will advocate for you within the firm, be the team you need, with the clients who love you; make sure those who need to know are aware that you are leveling up. And you want them on Team You. (I like to call this building the pie factory.)

The cool thing about that last option? If you are in the position to be an advocate for others, it is a power play for your own career. Your career will become infinitely more influential, and your own practice will have the legs to thrive, when you allow others to grow and own their expertise and role with clients.

Being the mentor and sponsor to help others on your team build great practices makes you look only better. And that puts you in a stronger position to work for the great clients you have, and the ones that will be showing up at your door.

Why discuss teams when the focus is supposed to be business development?

Within a firm, the natural progression up the ranks requires a mutual respect and flow of work and responsibility. Those who have attorneys with thriving (enviable) practices encourage others to work with them; they support the practice of others, whether by sharing origination, introductions, or clients, rather than trying to keep everything for themselves and never lending a helping hand.

If you are still reading, you have decided that it is worth acknowledging what got you here, while recognizing it is not what will get you to the next level. And that's exactly where you need to be because it means you're ready to make some changes and see what works for you.

There are just two choices here: one, wait it out and see if it gets better; or, two, be the one in control of your own practice.

You know my vote. If you stop waiting, you get to at least put things in motion to see the options and opportunities waiting for you, test and decide for yourself what fits, and change your mindset from stuck and pissed to up and out.

Activity:

Go back to your timeline and look. How much of what you remember, cherish, love, and respect in your career path were decisions someone else made for you; which ones did you actively engage in creating? Be honest with yourself. Even ones that seemed like luck or making the best out of a situation had you choosing to build relationships, show up as your best, and opt-in to opportunities that seemed to just pop out of nowhere. When you choose to step into the game, you are at least a part of the story.

Know and Own Your Value

I clearly remember the day sitting around a hotel suite with a team of attorneys in stiff navy suits, prepping for a pitch. Having gathered from around the country, everyone was poring over the details of the proposal, making sure we knew who was talking about what. When we got to my section, the work product I'd be delivering had attached to it a ginormous dollar amount. I was horrified and immediately offered up my work as the place to cut. We could lower my rate, blend the rate, or offer set-up discounts all under the guise of the economies of scale of my practice. This, I believed, would help the pitch, and emphasize my willingness to be a team player. That's when the senior partner seated across from me at a big, empty table, told me it was time to knock it off and own my worth. He continued to inform me that we would sit at that big, long table together for as long as it took me to own the value I brought to the table. And we did. For hours.

The gift that partner gave me cannot be understated. Even 15+ years ago, the number attached to my work was not small. Learning how to own it, and my worth, was a game changer.

You want to talk about confidence? Yeah, that went a long way in building it. I mean to pay that mindset shift forward.

The first step in owning your value is getting comfortable with your billable hour, the cost to work with you, and the investment a client makes to have you as the strategic thinking partner in the conversations with them.

Oh, the billable hour. Is there anything that creates a bigger internal worth conflict out there? If you haven't bumped into this bad boy yet, just wait until you move into this next practice stage. Remember when you were a new associate? You did the work, tried to learn, and wrote down your time. That was your job.

Your career has now evolved, your hourly rate seems to skyrocket, and suddenly you must defend how long it takes you to do something—and the dollar value to which it translates. You must defend it to clients and then you must defend it to yourself. What no one tells you as a fresh associate is that one day you will be the one to pick up the phone and explain why that rate is worth the value of your services. No one will believe you if your voice cracks with disbelief as you spew crappy logic out of your mouth because you, yourself, think it's as insane as the client.

Now, let's set aside whether there are alternative billing methods that may, or may not, be appropriate. As it turns out, it doesn't matter how you bill; you still are exchanging your expertise that takes time and energy for money. It's a hard pill to swallow.

The billable hour often creates additional conflict in how it's interpreted and taught to lawyers as they rise through the ranks. The primary conflict arises when every minute of your day must be billed; it must be used to bring in revenue, serve clients, and make money. This conjures up feelings of guilt and stress when you opt to scroll social media, take a break, or even a day off. You envision dollars flushing down the toilet; you wince in physical pain and tell yourself you can make it up down the road. Your time equals money, plain and simple.

This warped sense of the value of your time, coupled with having to ask a client to pay for it, makes you shudder. You've worked hard to get to this level of expertise and experience; yet when you look in the mirror, you can barely believe you have the right to a driver's license, let alone the ability to charge a three- to four-figure rate for just your knowledge. *You can't be that smart, right?*

How easy it is to forget that a lawyer's time is by and large spent thinking. Which means your knowledge is wrapped up like a little present with a fabulous bow. Your bright ideas and incredible words have a bigger associated price tag than anything slung into a Tiffany gift box, and that takes some getting used to. Talk about a pressure situation. Especially when clients want to talk about your rates (which feels like bad form, considering most of us were taught never to talk about money). You need to know how to handle it so you don't get flustered and end up creating a bigger mess than figuring out how to own the rates and value you bring.

Money, Oh, Money

If you want to watch attorneys squirm, ask them to talk about their own billable hour. If you want to turn up the heat, bring in an Ideal, and watch how the instinct to discount takes over their brains. Until you figure this stuff out, you'll do the same, squirm like you've committed a crime. An amazing new client asks how it works to work with you, and there you go, falling all over yourself, trying to brush away the hourly rate the firm has tacked onto your practice. You'll start trying to hedge the discounts and packages you can offer to reel them in, or the amount of time the project might take, to seem like the right choice. Just bring them in the door, and you can deal with the whole "payment" thing later.

This is a big mistake. Nothing causes more problems down the road than feeling like you are not getting paid the right value for the work, arguing with a client over a bill—or worse yet, spending your time trying to collect on that bill.

Before you can offer up your hourly rate without the hand-wringing theatrics, you gotta own it. I mean own it. And that requires grabbing a piece of paper and getting to work.

I've heard plenty of money mindset experts say that the best hourly rate to choose is the one that makes you feel like puking when you say it out loud. This assumes that you are setting your own rates and that this is just a fake-it-until-you-make-it moment. As though getting over the mindset issue simply requires that you push through monumental discomfort until you're spat out the other side into your comfort zone. But, until you recognize the value and worth you bring to the table, no amount of puking is going to make it easy to rattle off the investment to hire you as a trusted thinking partner. (Did you notice the shift to thinking about your work as a business investment that the client needs to make to meet their goal? Sneaky, right?)

Let's get to owning your value right up top.

Activity:

Grab a sheet of paper and put your hourly rate at the top of the page. I don't want your standard rate, average rate, or discounted rate. I want your "A Rate." The rest is yours to fill in with all the reasons you are worth every single penny of that rate. That's it. When you think you are done, tuck it away and take it out tomorrow. Read it and add to it. My suggestion is that you keep at this.[9]

---

[9] This is a Guide exercise. debfeder.com/guide.

Even after you start strutting into every room, emboldened by an hourly rate that matches the practice you own, this list will serve as your support system, something you can rely on when times get tough. Because they will. Someone will question one little thing, and you will wonder, *what if I charged just a smidge less? What would I be able to do if I . . . or, maybe this whole thing is crazy. Maybe I'm not worth it.*

The value piece allows you to get a little braver. When you know you have earned your stripes, that you have legit experience and expertise to back up your thoughts, you can share them more freely.

With all this heavy lifting upfront, you are now in the space to be in conversations, and get curious from a place of confidence, rather than fear.

Once your brain is in this game, and you have decided to take control of your own plans and pace, the connections, conversations, and steps you make matter. Because you are no longer on the practice path to nowhere train. You've got a firm hold and are owning a place in this game. Keep moving. This happens one connection and conversation at a time.

Just keep reading the list and reminding yourself that every step in your journey is another level of the amazing pedestal you are creating for your career. And you are standing on top of it. Owning it like you just lit the Olympic flame.

Step 2:

Know Thyself and Others

A Word on Conversations

Have you ever sat there in a conversation having an out-of-body experience? You know, your mouth is saying one thing, you hope it sounds intelligent, and your brain is racing around a million miles a minute, not sure what is happening.

Oh, it's just me; that's cool.

The last time this happened to me, I was looking for cell phone service in a dungeon of a hotel and Brené Brown was hanging out in the lobby before a speech. This is not a bad joke. It happened.

With no one else around, we ended up talking for a few minutes about her work and my work, which somehow led the conversation to twinkle lights in San Antonio. I remember saying that I couldn't come to a training she was hosting, and her explaining the importance of being there for the twinkle lights. The San Antonio holiday twinkle lights were worth it, she promised. I also remember looking around, wondering what in the world was going on.

Turns out, this is how authentic conversations come about. They just happen. I could have ignored her. I could have pretended to be on a call as I wildly waved my phone around for reception in the lobby. Instead, I said hello. And interesting things came of it.

Because of that conversation, I attended and completed The Daring Way™ program, which is based on the research of Dr. Brené Brown. Mind you, this wasn't in a twinkle-light-studded town, but I met incredible people at the training, nonetheless. I had this experience simply because I said hello.

It's the start of a conversation.

So, here's to kickstarting the discussion of networking.

Let's face it, the word "networking" may tempt you to throw this book somewhere on a bookshelf behind your old Torts textbook. It conjures images of shaking hands and racing between coffees, cocktail parties, and one more gross salad lunch. Somewhere along the way, you start to get hives just imagining the cringe-worthy conversations and the rapid-fire pace this type of networking brings up. You shake your head knowing there is no way to cram one more thing into the busy practice already on your desk (because you still must get everyone else's work done while going out and trying to find your own). The idea of engaging in any of these conversations might as well be a nonstarter up for discussion.

Please stop.

At its core, a conversation is simply two people discussing an idea, thought, or opinion. How you implement the remaining parts of relationship building, and the format of conversations you focus on, has a whole lot to do with you and less to do with the formal right and wrong of getting into client conversations.

Some of you love a big, crowded function—you walk out feeling energized; others of you refuse anything that requires leaving the joggers and ponytail behind. Some love a Zoom meeting; others would be happy to never have another remote meeting again; others still want to double down on the email conversation. No matter what, there is only one guiding star.

You must be you.

Examples and directions aside, always circle back to the fact that when you come up with your networking rules (which is what we're going to do), it comes down to you. The reason you write these rules down is a step-in accountability to yourself.[10]

When you honor and respect how you want to go about this, you follow your own guidelines; you remember where and how you decided to be brave, show up, and join the conversations.

---

[10] Yup. This is in the Guide.

Once this happens, we can discuss what works for you, after hello.

You Before Them

When I was in college, a boyfriend invited me to his parents' lake house for the weekend. My first such getaway with a "beau," I was ready, armed with the perfect hostess gift and my best chatty self. Well, this changed the moment we walked in the door and the stories started flowing about the high-maintenance significant others the siblings had brought home. Each story revolved around food; the whole family chimed in to mock and tease each other about the picky eaters of the past. I knew I didn't want to be in that category. (Mind you, this was in the middle of my vegetarian phase, which lasted about six months—or until this trip when I had to rethink everything.) What happened next? Me, a massive plate of ribs, and the eyes of the entire family watching me.

You can imagine the internal conversation I was having, yet I had quickly lost sight of me, and who I was, and just wanted to please this guy and his big family. I didn't just eat those very non-vegetarian animal ribs, I dove in. So much so, that I convinced myself that I loved every bite. Until about an hour later . . .

Now, as you might intuit, those ribs were the first hint that this was not the relationship for me. Without much effort, I took on the persona that someone else wanted of me.

It's similar to what you do when targeting the cool client. You try your level best to be who you think they want you to be—from the clothes you wear, to the restaurants you choose. From there, you try to sound like the cool kid. All of it making you show up flat, not terribly interesting. Because you aren't being you.

Again, clients are looking to build real relationships and work with real people. Which means you must be just that: real.

Now, I know what you are thinking. *I'm good with that.* But do you know your preferences, your likes, dislikes, and the kind of conversations you want to have? Not just what you think is hip or happening, but what energizes you, and how to talk about it?

This does not require a strengths analyzer, or any serious professional analysis, but it does require paying attention. To you. That's right, you must reintroduce yourself to you.

As an adult, it's valid that your preferences, energy, and perspective have changed. You are not the person who started out on this journey. For the purposes of this chapter, forget about what clients you have, which ones you want, and which ones pay the bills. Tell that lengthy checklist in your head to relax for a few. To get to know yourself, you need to let all the obligations rest for a moment.

This may sound good, but it's not without traps. Traps may feel like mind games. Like when the universe seemingly throws you a curve ball when the practice you are certain you hate suddenly rewards you with the deal of the decade. You flip-flop between utter horror and pure elation, knowing this is a decision moment trying to trick you into staying with the old, while holding off on the big dreams.

Or, what about the client from whom you have spent six months detangling yourself, who suddenly shows up at your door, acting nice, and offering you the case of a lifetime? Your brain loves to tell you that person has changed; it will be different this time; you can't pass it up—and before you know it, you're grabbing at those docs before you have the chance to take two deep breaths. Trust me, pause and take those deep breaths. Ask a few questions. Make an informed decision before thinking the stars have finally aligned and people have changed.

Other times traps appear in those around us. Some will want you to stay your predictable self. They will either reward the old choices or be pissed at you for showing up a little differently, forcing you to triage their annoyance.

You may even be a hinderance. You're bound to experience moments where you feel too fuzzy to figure it all out, making you wonder if this whole getting centered and grounded in you-being-you is worth it.

It is. To that end, the following is a list of some big questions you'll want to answer—and you need to do so all at once. As you start to marinate on them, jot your ideas; notice what resonates, and feel free to fill in the margins with your thoughts. If a question annoys you, pay attention to that, too. You'll later circle back to those things that make you bristle.

Answer these questions in reverse order:

- What are your big goals right now all about—what do the ones bringing in a book of business feed into? Is it money, a promotion, the security of the position? What is behind the goal?

- What do you want your practice to be known for? Why did you get into this in the first place? Why have you stuck around? What do you secretly love when no one is around, and you don't have to complain?

- What do you want for your life—what's the life you love living look like? Think big and bold. Dream about your future and make sure it has a voice in this discussion.

- What do you want for yourself? Kind of like that college philosophy course that made you ponder the meaning

> of life for a semester, go deep. Get centered and allow yourself to remember what's important to you. This should anchor everything else, from this point forward. [This is the starting point . . . work up from here.]

With all this thinking about what you want, your goal is not to fall into the trap of chasing after the glittery practice. As it turns out, my mom (oh, and Shakespeare) was right: all that glitters is not gold.

It's a misnomer to aim for the hot persona of the moment. It would be like turning me into a shampoo spokesperson on IG. I mean, I like shampoo just as much as the next person, but I'd have a hard time mustering the right level of enthusiasm. Not happening. And I'm not going to be one of those cool kids putting out reels about their morning routine. First, I don't care about morning routines; second, it would be absurd for me to film myself drinking coffee and nagging my kids. (Also, I'm pretty sure I just used reels in the wrong way, which should speak volumes.)

In other words, before you start trying to emulate others and make your world the envy of the firm partner meetings, know what you are chasing. When you go after the cool stuff, just because it looks cool, it can often feel like a bust (or quickly deflating balloon left at our feet). Know the difference between trendy and what you could nerd out on all day long and get everyone else excited about with your infectious enthusiasm.

Because it turns out infectious enthusiasm is the cool stuff and the envy of everyone in the office.

The key is to avoid trying to be, or create, cool. When you do, you lose track of the voice you're listening to. When you get caught up in that story of what's trendy or acceptable—in yourself and those around you—you miss out on so much. It's easy to think that no issues can sully this impressive zone. Yet, regardless of the cool factor (yours or your clients'), there's often a good dose of some rather uncool stuff.

You must be self-aware enough to know what works for you and what doesn't, apart from the shimmering imagery. Ask yourself: Are you seeing things as they are, or have you been taken hostage by the need to seem enchanting?

Activity:

Here are two writing exercises to make sure you are thinking straight when you're considering if you want to work with a client or not, or if you're fooling yourself into believing you do:

1. *Take five minutes to journal about why this client or work is important to you: what do you love about the work? What energizes you? Separate the shiny from reality. Is it still cool if the business name changes, or the person in charge is suddenly not who you expected? Consider*

it from all angles. Label this: "The Important Stuff."

2. *Keep a notepad with a page dedicated to stuff that annoys you. Spend one or two days writing down what you notice. Some of it might be tasks, others might be qualities in people. Doesn't matter. But it does inform you of your boundaries. Label this: "The Annoyance List."*

Try and notice upfront when someone's glitter is just gloss on top of problems. This will help you pay attention.

Rose-colored glasses set on the credenza (hell, dropped in the trash), how do you fill your roster with Ideals once you've done the work of identifying them?

Stop Chasing Clients

When you don't show up as yourself, you think chasing the cool kids is the way to the top. Begging to get invited to the party is lowering yourself and your position within a relationship such that you are not entering on even ground. Nothing is more off-putting than someone being overly eager, to the point of desperation. Stop stalking your dream clients. Showing up where they have happy hour, always sidling up to the bar with them, is weird. Leaving ten voicemails and twenty emails begins to raise a red flag. Not to mention, oftentimes those amazing clients you chased for years, turn out to be not-so-amazing once you land them and must deal with their projects.

So, get comfortable being you. When you are centered and grounded in who you are—what you bring to the table—and you're confident in your practice, you stop chasing. When you do, you can start building and relying on systems that have the good clients reaching out to you. You know where you want to show up, and you feel confident being in those spaces and places (whether in person or hanging out online in places like LinkedIn).

And remember, you and your Ideal will change.

No matter where you are in your practice, your Ideal will change because you are changing. Even reading this book is putting little brain synapses in play that trigger ideas and plans without you even realizing. Not only does your career path inform where you are going, the market changes. The lesson? Don't get too cozy thinking this is something that is "done"; rather, get comfortable with the habit and evolution of finding, learning about, and testing out clients with your ideal plan.

The better you get at understanding you for who you are, and how to see Ideals for who they are, the better you can engage in conversations. The more authentic the conversations, the better you're able to show up for the right people, in the right way. The point of this whole thing is that you build a book without having to chase. You and your expertise shine on its own. Your days of running after clients with hopes that they might notice you in the crowd are over. Agreed?

Circling back: you need to know you.

Circling back to where we began: be comfortable and confident; show up as you; you gotta know yourself. It's a big ask, I know.

For so long, I used to think it was all about helping lawyers and professionals get courageous and brave about what's next. It turns out, we often don't know what we want "next." Having left little parts of ourselves in the hallways of the office as we race from one project and obligation to another, we haven't a clue what the next phase of our career looks like. We're unable to see past learning to do this thing called having a private law practice. But until you know yourself, what you want to build and are willing to bet on it, your brain will keep tricking you into thinking the scramble for others is necessary, making it feel nearly impossible to give it up for the hope of something better.

With that, let's go find you in the rubble that's been left behind while you launch your career.

Activity:

This one starts with paper and some colored pencils. Trust me. It works. You pick the colored pencils only because your life isn't meant to be displayed on spreadsheets, or in black and white. It's meant to be seen in technicolor.

A few exercises to get to know you:

1. *Plan your perfect day. Not giving in to anyone else, but you. And not what you are supposed to like. In other words, don't default to binging Netflix or reading Dostoyevsky. Instead, tap into what you truly like. What fills your bucket? Draw it out. Brainstorm. Dream. Cut out pictures. Whatever it takes. Want to go the extra mile? Make a reservation for lunch where you would go on this perfect day. Grab a friend and make it happen.*

2. *Know your favorite foods. Not just the leftovers your kids allow you to nibble on at the end of the meal. Chicken nuggets cannot be on the list. Or ribs. Making decisions for yourself matters. Starting with what you like to eat.*

3. *Understand when you work best. What time of day does the clock fly? When does it feel like the second hand has moved to a crawl and you are certain it's broken? Notice your rhythms in the day.*

4. *When was the last time you smiled at work? What was going on? Give this one a whole lot of time. Notice when you smile and when others are smiling with you. It matters.*

Notice, there's no question about what sucks. It's not about what you don't like. This is owning what is you being allowed to be you. Practice with the small stuff, and you can start to own the big stuff that comes with it.

Example: Me.

1. My perfect day starts well before dawn with a steaming cup of coffee, in my favorite mug that is often a little hot to hold but keeps in the heat. Preferably the blend I once found in Québec City.

2. My favorite meal is perfectly cooked roasted chicken. Nothing fancy. But perfect flavor. Second favorite is the amazing moussaka down the street. It is just comfort and heaven wrapped in a baked wonderful-ness every time.

3. Working my best depends on the task. Mornings are for thinking and writing. Weekends are time for big paper and strategy.

4. I smile every single day at work. So much so that my kids are convinced that my work consists of gossiping with friends. They haven't figured out that I love my clients, and my work involves conversations, and a whole lot of levity and laughter.

How about you; want a challenge? Send me a note (deb@debfeder.com) telling me your answers, or better yet, pop on LinkedIn and share a little bit about what you do so lots of people can get to know you. Pick one piece of your work and perspective to share.

The Myth of the Ideal Client

Imagine a rooftop lined with experts. Each one with a megaphone, and they all keep saying:

> "Know your ideal client!"
>
> "Hunt them down!"
>
> "Know what handbags and sports teams they love!"
>
> "Keep your pitch in your pocket!"
>
> "Make them know you!"
>
> "They will call!"

Not sure if this is the chimney sweep scene in *Mary Poppins* gone wrong, or the ghosts in *Field of Dreams* . . . either way, you need to shut this messaging down.

The core problem with all this loud noise is multifold. But let's begin with the notion of "ideal." It's time to run that misnomer to ground.

Before I married, I had this idea that there was an ideal guy. Twenty years later I don't remember all the details, but I am certain it included the types of books he read, the music he enjoyed, the dinners he would pick with me in mind, and his complete obsession with understanding and respecting my career.

Then I met Andrew.

He picked the worst possible restaurant for our first date, not thinking that a busy lawyer would be crazy annoyed at a mediocre restaurant twenty-five minutes away when awesome spots surrounded her apartment. Not to mention, Phish popped from the speakers, which made me want to flee through the kitchen door. (You should probably know that I go for pop-country-folk blends.)

Andrew is decidedly not a travel planner, so he bailed on honeymoon planning. He is, however, a willing explorer and up for an adventure, which earned him two points for attitude. He was equally busy building his own business, and while having a very healthy respect for my career, my plans blew his plans for some idyllic life of a perfectly clean house and pleasant wife at 5 p.m. every day out of the water. All this goes to show that we needed to meet somewhere close to the middle to build this amazing life we've got going on today.

My husband certainly didn't start out checking some crazy "ideal" list in my head. He was and is just a regular person with preferences and goals that occasionally intersect with mine. And that works just fine.

Ideals are the same way. They're just people who don't always operate the way you'd like or expect. You have a big list in your head of what they are going to look and act like, but you'd be surprised how often they refuse to tick the fantasy boxes.

Your Big Wish List

Can you remember starting your practice (or even law school) and dreaming of "it" clients? You imagined it would be a modern-day *L.A. Law* combined with a Netflix docu-series. Exhilarating, fast-paced, and endlessly fascinating. From that moment on, you started creating the practice of your dreams in your head. Your brain got busy creating forty-five-minute episodes of clients begging for your expertise, calling on you in their moments of big decisions, serious strategy needs, and paying outrageous bills with a gift basket of gratitude. The companies they worked for—and their values, products, and line offerings—all aligned with your political and social beliefs to a T. Your dreams ran wild, layering the substantive work with images of blue jeans, ping pong table strategy sessions, and cool wine dinners. Because, while you envisioned yourself out there in the world doing good, you were also having fun. And those characters—I mean, clients—always respected your priorities and boundaries. They even sent flowers when they heard you'd caught a cold. Maybe even some chicken soup.

These clients do exist, just not at first. Kind of like how Andrew is now that guy who loves nothing more than entertaining when my retreat participants join us for dinner in our home; and he knows exactly what I give a shit about. Because it turns out he is that guy.

But we've fallen prey to the concept of airbrushed, perfect clients thanks to our colleagues' egos, social media, and our brains.

Let's face it. Doing well in school involved hierarchy. The competitive atmosphere started back in third grade with how well you knew your multiplication tables relative to everyone else in the class. It never got much better. College admissions, the LSAT, and the first day of law school when the professor started making you show off (otherwise called answering questions) in front of your future colleagues—it was all about proving that you were smarter than everyone else.

Fast-forward, now you've got offices filled with people tossing around statements like, "The clients just come to me"; "My clients can't stop gushing about how much they love me and about how they'd never replace me"; "I'm the youngest partner to have a book this big." Hopefully, your senses are refined enough to recognize this as psych-out puffery. Yet, you're bound to fall prey to the idea that your colleagues are working with Ideals, and you're stuck at your desk doing lousy work for everyone else, while the wine is flowing at the cocktail parties you weren't invited to.

Social media plays an even bigger role. Pinterest pins picture-perfect office settings where clients greet you with craft coffees and gift sets to onboard your support. (I mean, I'm not into Birken bags, but I would take one if offered.) Facebook promotes teams hugging it out on the beach with cocktails to celebrate the winning verdict. Instagram shows professionals working from some cottage in Europe with a host of clients sending virtual high-fives over Zoom. TikTok makes you long for the team that's willing to put together a viral dance. And LinkedIn . . . well, it has it all wrapped into one.

All this messaging, along with that outstanding group of "friends" from school and summer associate wine-dine moments, may lead you to believe that the key to the perfect practice is filling it with Ideals. And the path to that is staying true from Day One to your boundaries, beliefs, and big-ass goals.

Only, you can't tell what's real, thanks to a ginormous airbrush.

Keeping these fantasies alive will block any chance you have of building a practice with Ideals. Instead, you'll keep complaining incessantly about everything that defies this delusion. Telling yourself that the only way to fill your practice with these unicorns is by staying frozen until it somehow happens one day, convincing yourself you are playing the long game. It turns out you are playing the waiting-for-sometime-probably-never game.

The Perfect Setups

Here are a few other fantasies that need to be cast aside if you want a shot at developing a solid practice and a love affair with hunting for Ideals. They're more like perfect setups that don't exist anywhere outside of Instagram:

1. Sophisticated deals that can be replicated without effort or thought (fifteen years of practicing . . . and still waiting for the time when you don't have to start at the beginning). High-end work requires high-end thinking, every time. This isn't plug-and-play type stuff.

2. Teams that know the exact moment to include you in conversations without ever wasting your time on excess calls or emails. (Does anyone get this one right?!)

3. Work that simply fits between the hours of 9 and 5—and, of course, has a healthy respect for holidays and family time. (I had a deal erupt while going into labor and my boss was in a foreign country . . . trust me, no

timing is perfect in this world.)

4. Cases that have perfectly organized files and a great team ready to answer your every question. (If you are waiting for your desk and inbox to be organized, you might as well go to the office supply store to see if unicorns are being sold on the shelf.)

Hope for Them, and They Will Come

Now, let's get to the other garbage coming out of those rooftop megaphones.

The presumption is that you know yourself, your practice, and with whom you want to work, including the right details to get started. But rarely do you have a good enough idea of who this Ideal is, other than your shiny-glossy-airbrushed fantasy that has you holding a beer and negotiating under the umbrella on the beach.

Here's another problem. It's all well and good to know what type of office your Ideals work in, but that's pretty much where the specifics end for most lawyers. You should be able to demonstrate a fairly deep level of understanding regarding the client. When the specifics are vague, hitting a home run (or a touchdown) with any business development strategy will happen despite the strategy, not because of it. It's basically aiming at a missing target.

What are the details? A full description of the industry and where it is growing (and what it evolved from). The company's big ten-year plans, and the daily annoyances that keep everyone dragged down. The projects, cases, and priorities on their desks; what they want to have someone else manage (not just the stuff you want to manage). Not to mention their legal strategy and how it blends with those big business goals.

One more thing. Just like you might be a bit vague on how this looks for you, don't expect a client to know all this about themselves. Whether you're in-house or private practice, this exercise is critical to get the people around you to support the work and goals you need done. Otherwise, you are sitting up late at night, wondering how it all landed on your plate, wishing it was different, unsure of how to distinguish yourself in the company. How do I know this to be true? Because I have been there. And I know it can be different.

Back to the trap of being too fuzzy with the details to know what you're after. This lack of clarity shows up in several ways:

1. Your description of this Ideal is broad at best. Startups. Business owners. Insurance companies. Banks. CEOs. With all due respect, none of these descriptions amount to anything. In other words, they attract no one.

2. You attract the wrong ones because you haven't clarified your language. You never realized that the Ideals you are

describing could mean THAT kind of client. What do I mean? I once allowed someone else to help target my client base, bringing me a host of potters wanting me to help them get business. Potters? Yet, when I stepped back, the client description could have fit the same job description. Clearly, this was a major miss. Let's just say we never used that strategy again, and it made me go back and clarify the language and focus of my Ideal.

3. You wait because you think you can't move forward until you sweat every, minute detail. Since you can't describe Ideals, you choose to hold back until your big plan fits perfectly together—which is on the other side of never.

So, there you sit, stuck, telling yourself that the clients you really want to work with are working with others, or they don't like you, or they're wandering out in the forest and can't find you. You blame the strategists, firm, colleagues, and clients. All because you can't see the one problem standing in your way, which is you haven't stopped chasing unicorns long enough to be with the clients, referral partners, and colleagues that are in your space.

Let that sink in for a minute. Instead of chasing after the illusion, dive in and start to figure out what resonates and fits, and where you and your practice are right now.

Start with What You've Got

So, am I telling you that there's no such thing as an Ideal, that your job is to accept your current client base and their messy humanity, that you just need to stop complaining and suck it up?

Absolutely not. I'm going to tell you where to find your Ideals. But, before I do, you've got to get yourself ready. You may not be ready to have the kind of curious, confident conversations that build the right book of business quite yet.

At its core, the Ideal—the client and ensuing relationship—is an adult relationship founded upon high levels of trust. Until you learn how to develop that, you're probably going to fail. Your bright shiny clients are going to disappoint you, and vice versa.

While I could write an entire book on this, we're going to distill down the problem with trust-building so you can enjoy your client relationship and not lose your gourd. That big fantasy of yours—what your Ideal will say and do, the flowers they will send, etc.—jumps past the getting to know you, messy middle, and trust-building phases. You're imagining some "end point" that never exists. Because when things start to get cozy, the deal or team blows up and you need to have a solid foundation from which to pivot and respond (rather than react in the midst of chaos).

Most clients, ideal or otherwise, do not walk in with high levels of trust; they walk in hoping someone is going to handle their problems. They show up stressed, worried, and frazzled. Lawyers are skeptical to begin with, so the client relationship is likely to start rocky because you don't exude come-rest-on-me charm. This serves as a good reminder; you aren't going to have a high level of trust from the beginning. It's something that builds over time.

You build that trust from many angles. Answering the phone and smiling in a meeting are the basics. As the relationship deepens and expands over time, the trust becomes more engrained, and the grip of control (on both sides) loosens. But the conversation progression starts here, at that first hello.

You build further trust by getting the work done, at the quality, speed, and tone required by the client. Of course, trust is a two-way street. You trust that the client will give you all the information, understand the work involved, and know how and when to pull the emergency cord.

While the trust is building, you'll be able to spot "idealness" in the client. If you start getting judgy right off the bat, you will never pick up the phone for that so-called second date with the client.

The Messy Middle

What if, instead of hunting for Ideals, you got comfortable working with the relationships around you to figure out what you want; what if you started befriending the discomfort of the messy middle?

Your ideal client may not be out there, but sitting next to you, waiting for you to notice. Seriously, what if you are already working with your Ideal, maybe just not doing the ideal work? It could be a current or former client, with other projects or new work for which they're trying to figure out what to do; it could be a referral partner that is tightly connected to the exact Ideal with whom you are wanting to build out your practice. As it turns out, this isn't so farfetched; Ideals tend to be sitting with us, right next to us, or just a couple seats away, more often than not. And they are waiting for you.

While current clients may or may not be a great fit for you, they are in the perfect spot to help you learn, validate, and strategize. Practicing progressing the conversation with them can help you figure out precisely who your Ideals are, what they do, specifically, and how they work. What makes them perfect for you, or perfect enough, and what makes for kryptonite.

This approach to client acquisition and retention works especially well when we are bound to make this relationship the most important thing in the world. As it turns out, keeping current clients happy (or at least pleasantly satisfied) is pretty much your job description. Which makes talking to them and understanding them not just good for your career, it solidifies your current relationship (because it comes off as giving a damn) . . . making this strategy a win-win for everyone.

There is another by-product of easing up and getting into relationship-building conversations with people you aren't just chasing down the halls. It allows you to relax. Take a deep breath. Stop trying to sound like *Black's Law Dictionary* and show up as a human. Because clients are just people wanting to work with real people. Only then will you be in the mental space to clearly see the situation and begin to figure out what kind of clients you're meant to work with.

If you're scratching your head because you're not exactly sure what I mean . . .

Client Relationships Are Just Relationships

Much like the dating world, you get into a new client relationship and grab your rose-colored glasses on the way out the door.

You fall hook, line, and sinker for the "sure thing." It's like an adrenaline hit for the promise of billable hours, something to do, and being wanted. No matter the size of the question, the minute you get that first email or call, you feel important. Which somehow translates to "respected." Jumping on the client bus, you jam out to "Celebration."

Since you never pause to consider whether these new clients line up with your goals, priorities, or practice, this is often the point where things head south (at least in hindsight when we try to figure out what went wrong). Celebrations have quickly turned to constant emails, cryptic requests, and phone calls that leave you scrambling out the door. What was amazing now feels like a slap in the face, making you wonder how such a great client turned on you so quickly.

When these relationships fail to play out the way we envisioned (and it happens), we default to anger, resentment, frustration, and/or exhaustion. That's why, before you continue your search for the Ideal, you need to get comfortable with the fact that your client relationships are as messy as any other human connection. Because that's what they are: relationships.

So, instead of looking for amazing clients who make you sing from the start, circle back to the first hello. Allow yourself to build the base of a trusting relationship through basic conversation. The smallest of projects and moments count big time here. This is where you move into proving yourself, focusing on the quality of your work and advice. (This is where you start scoring big in the trust game, especially if you are the only one who embraces the small projects with the same enthusiasm as the career-making billable-hour-busting big ones.) Are you capable of showing up how they want, and does it match how you want to be seen? Following up gives you a mutual sense of how the pace of work, decisions, and next steps work in an ever-changing relationship.

The key is in the balance: stay present; pay attention; ask great questions—to the clients in front of you and to yourself. Yes, you're building trust. But you're also practicing discernment.

Even in the smallest of moments, there is a chance to build trust, figure out if you are a working-match, and start to "train" the client on how you can best represent and support them in the next big project. Together, you work to find mutual respect, boundaries, and resources. Common goals, they do exist.

Decide to Be Interested and Interesting

Finding your Ideals, and yourself, through curious, confident conversations means you can be the very best judge of whether the people around you are worth the hustle.

But first . . .

Have you ever looked around and wondered how you got to be so boring? I have. Recently, in fact. I love my work. I love my family. I love my days. But when things got quiet, I found myself filling my time binge-watching television. Sure, I work out, and I have friends. But there was this nagging void post-pandemic begging me to fill my bucket with something more. I was no longer interesting. I was bored with myself.

Trust me, when you're bored with yourself, you tend to be boring to others, and there goes curiosity and confidence right out the window.

You can't realize this and not decide to do something about it. I started with shutting down my computer and turning off my phone at a much earlier hour than I had in years and finding my way back to wandering around bookstores. Travel planning began to be fun, rather than a logistical nightmare and constant headache. And I remembered how much I loved playing gin rummy with my Grandma Ruth; now I love playing it with my son. I started getting interesting again. It's a work in process. But it has transformed how I feel about myself and my days and has brought a depth to my work that has me invigorated and exuding new energy.

Filling up your bucket does have a direct connection to your work. It gives new energy to the conversations; interesting stuff to share. You can pay attention to the nuances in the small talk of others because you are aware of what's going on in the world around you. From the hot new restaurant to the trendy app everyone is buzzing about—you are interested and interesting. Even when you have no clue (seriously, one of these days I will understand TikTok), you know enough to ask (and want to know the answers to) great questions.

Even if you get into a conversation with an Ideal, not much is going to happen if you always stick to talking about the weather. Sure, it's a fine line. You want them to know about the value, perspective, and experience you bring to the table, without sounding like a walking billboard or slick sales team; you want to seem interested, without looking or feeling like a stalker.

Put the Pitch in the Trash

Years ago, I had a client email me in a bind because she wasn't sure what to do with the signature piece of advice her internal big law team kept preaching: "Always keep your pitch in your pocket." Since it felt more like an awkward weight in her pocket, my advice was simple: throw that conversation stopper in the trash and start engaging in good conversations.

Now, to clarify, I'm not talking a formal pitch to which you have been invited. Say "yes" when such opportunities present themselves (and prep like hell). The pitch to which I'm referring sounds something like this: "I am a business lawyer who handles my clients' needs and the one you want on your team." One, yuck. Two, I have no clue what this even means, who you help, or why you are offering to take the client without knowing more. Some call these elevator speeches, or one-lines. Doesn't matter, they fail to resonate and leave everyone feeling kind of gross.

Hence, the reason "always keep your pitch in your pocket" is lousy advice:

1. A canned intro is not a conversation. It is a memorized speech that often lands like a lead balloon.

2. When you walk into a cocktail party ready to share your "pitch," you forget to listen, making this a one-way conversation that your Ideal doesn't care about.

3. You sound like everyone else. Blending in isn't the plan here.

4. You are so focused on getting this one line in, you don't pay attention to anything going on around you.

5. The moment to learn about the client (and treat them like a human being) is lost. You missed it.

Unfortunately, far too many have been given this lousy advice, leaving clients stuck listening to rambling attorneys trying to sound like they know everything about everything, while boring everyone to tears. This approach will not attract business. This is not a curious, confident conversation; this is torture. You don't want to be that person or stuck in that situation.

If you are that person, chances are good you didn't want to become a talking head; you may barely recognize yourself—and you're not quite sure how you got to be *that* awkward. But you've got to change because talking heads are awkward AF.

To get out of this quandary, you must figure out two things: how you got here and what to talk about. You're out of practice when it comes to natural conversation; that, it seems, is the *how*. The conversations you do have don't seem to go anywhere. So, what do you talk about? To start, get cozy with a new way of talking to and connecting with others.

Be interested and interesting. (Like that drumbeat?) Those are the guides to engaging in real conversations that aren't so slimy.

How to Get Interested

It's all about using incredible listening skills partnered with great questions. Don't simply prep your next joke or response in the banter, but actively listen and hear what everyone around you is saying. Pick up on the social cues and understand the nuances involved. (That's kind of the advanced class, but you'll get there.)

Getting interested in small talk situations means asking good questions. And these questions can evolve into market research, by the way. Here are a few examples:

The Introduction:

Conversation stopper: I am a lawyer. Practice securities.

Conversation starter: What kind of projects are you working on these days?

The Stepping into Conversation:

Conversation stopper: What office are you in?

Conversation starter: I am working on putting together a dinner list for when I hit the other offices, which one are you located out of (and where am I eating)?

The Gold Standard:

Conversation stopper: I'm in international arbitration and focus on only speaking to or caring about someone with a $500mm portfolio and who dines on sardines.

Conversation starter: I am working on understanding [_______________], and am curious what you are seeing with your clients?

Now that you have started getting interested, you need some other things to talk about. Question after question only goes so far—you have to be someone who's interesting to talk with.

Be Interesting

There are many ways you can move from your desk, out into the real world, to learn a thing or two to make yourself more interesting. Here are a few to get you started:

1. Hobbies. Do you have one? Do you want one? What are the little things you used to do when you were not working? Think playing cards, sewing, gardening, running . . . anything that you do just because it's fun.

This is the easiest stuff to talk about.

2. Pop culture. These are the Netflix binge-watching shows, documentaries, sporting events and updates, and whatever makes the hot splashy headlines. Yes, even the TikTok fads are worthy of knowing about if you happen to stumble upon the information.

3. Your work. Even though you don't want to sound like a pitch machine or the encyclopedia, if going "all in" on the cool facts and latest cases is your thing, then share away. When you light up and want to talk about it, so do others.

4. Snacks and stuff. People love to talk about food. Whether you are standing in front of the buffet or debating the best coffee in town, it is a universal conversation starter.

5. Colleges and hometowns. There is nothing more fun than talking about college rivalries and stories from where you grew up. Do you want me to start talking about Iowa . . .? What about my days of getting lost at football games in the Big House?

Hopefully, you get the idea. People love to talk about stuff. They can relate. It's easy. And if you light up talking about it, the conversation will flow.

Find the Intersection

You're interested in your clients. You're working on being an interesting human being. Now it pays to find the intersection between the two so you can communicate in a friendly, yet relevant fashion. Spend ten minutes on the internet looking around; find a publication that intersects what you find interesting—one that has just the right tone of smarts and entertainment, so you want to read it and share ideas with those you're building relationships with. A few of my personal favorites: *Fast Company, The Week, Ted Talks, The Wall Street Journal*, and *The New York Times*. Not for any particular purpose, and in no particular order, I just find good stuff waiting for me in each of these.

When you see something interesting you would like to share . . . wait for it . . . follow through and send it to someone you think might find it interesting and/or relevant. Potential clients. Referral partners. Colleagues you want to bring you onto the deal teams or next big case. Or cool people you met at the networking event.

When you think that you only need to talk to and nurture someone when there is a direct connection to dollars on the origination sheets, you are cutting off opportunity before it begins.

For those that would rather keep the connections to email, this is a great strategy. Using articles, videos, and updates to strengthen a connection works (kind of like magic). You aren't bothering them, and they aren't obligated to give you a ton of time, yet you are showing very clearly that you paid attention and were thinking about them when you ran across the "resource."

Need an idea? Any of the music documentaries currently streaming out there. They're infused with great lessons; pop culture enough to be interesting; intellectual enough to not be total fluff. There's no need to suggest anyone dive into a law review article or break down one more case. It strikes a solid tone in many a networking situation.

Side note: Don't send random nonsense. Whatever you send, make a connection to a past conversation.

Here is a simple template to get it done by email:

> Hey [John]—
> I hope all is well! I saw this article about time hacks, and it reminded me of the discussion we were having the other day about whether the hacks are worth it or not. Just curious if you think any of these make the cut. Looking forward to your thoughts. Deb

Or:

> Hey [John]-
> Just saw this update on [insert legal issue]. Wanted

> to make sure it had come across your desk. Looking forward to your thoughts. Reach out if I can get you any resources to help in putting these guidelines into action. Hope all is well. Deb

Notice how the second example comes close to offering up your services, but in a more subtle way. Also, if you choose to use one of these templates, remember to read the room, and make sure the emails sound like you (not me).

The Practical Application: Small Talk

Did you know one of the biggest stressors is being forced to make small talk? This also happens to be where you set the tone, personality, and start warming up the discussion. The idea of chit-chat or meaningless banter is positively terrifying for many, yet the simplest opportunity to build connection and trust without having to go "all in" on anything. When you are present, aware, and engaged, it resonates with those who are also sick of the grind; it gives a glimpse into your character and personality. Both of which are like fireworks for clients looking for someone with whom they can quickly build trust and confidence.

There are two parts to mastering small talk: what to say (go back to that "be interesting" list) and what to pay attention to. Unfortunately, you may be worrying so much about what to say, you don't pay attention. When you flip this, you will find easy topics and conversations waiting for you.

Paying attention to the micro-moments is key. Micro-moments are:

- The idle conversation at the beginning of a negotiation session.
- People talking about the weather, office supplies, restaurants, sports.
- Old friends with lots of shared stories—or the fact that everyone in the room is new.
- The random complaint about life that someone fires off when they don't even realize they are talking out loud.
- People who ramble off on a side comment, but veer back to the topic. Those side comments are still sitting in their brains, wanting a conversation, at the right time.

The person who stays to the end and helps clean off the table is usually the one who tunes in to this conversation-building fodder.

So, ask yourself this: What are those I work with frequently talking about at the beginning of each discussion? Practice paying attention. When you key in on these topics, you can incorporate them into your approach so you don't have to come up with something off the cuff (which can make you look out to lunch).

Solution: Give Yourself a Job

You know the shy kid that comes to school and the teacher gives that student the job of passing out papers? The teacher is on to something. The teacher knows if the students who aren't all that comfortable walking into the room have something to do, they'll find their place as they "work."

The same goes for you and walking into the big networking room. It applies to all conversations, big and small. And it's super simple.

Be curious.

No need to worry about your pitch or elevator speech. No need to spend hours rehearsing in the mirror. Simply get crazy curious. Start thinking about conversations like mini research projects that allow you to gather data. When you start to hear themes and ideas, it allows you to expand the conversation, build bridges between people, and add texture to your own thoughts and ideas. Most of all, it gives you a job. Something to focus your brain on, rather than the nerves of walking into the room. No longer hyper-focused on your outfit, your conversation skills, or the results of the night, you get to relax, and drive the conversation.

Pay attention to what you learn. You'll use it later.

Oh, and don't beat anyone down with so many questions their head spins. This approach cuts off the connection; rather than making you seem interested it makes you appear to be selling something, and it lands wrong.

The legal industry gets a bad rap. Mocked for heartless actions, ruthless negotiations, and made-for-tv dramas where there is little more than screaming and throwing stuff, which has little resemblance to the real life of a lawyer. In addition, clients are stuck listening to bad pitches like pick-up lines in a made-for-television movie, while lawyers spend hours trying to look shiny and smart. And if you plan to get into the who-is-smartest contest, you will almost inevitably lose.

Chaotic days, old habits of pointing the finger at everyone else, and genuine fear of being the awkward one in the room, creates a bad circular system that holds everyone back. Instead, you want to bring humanity to the crowd.

To have great conversations and network like a pro, the answer is simple. Be a kind human being. Be the one who pays attention to other people and is genuine in giving a hoot about them. Hold a door open; say "good morning"; be reasonable in your requests and demands. Advocate fiercely, while staying human. Be that person. Not only is it the right thing to do, but clients find it refreshing, interesting, and engaging.

You can still network the way you want; it just needs to involve human conversations with relevant follow-ups. Which, by the way, should reduce the awkwardness factor by about a thousand percent.

Remember, you are using conversations not just to grab new clients and billable hours, you are building relationships. Those great friendships built over study groups and late-night work sessions may have fallen by the wayside as you worked with your head down, no time for connection. But humans are meant to connect. You are meant to build friendships. And they take work. Show up. Be open. Recognize that you never know whether you are building a great client, referral partner, or new member of your book club. No matter the outcome, the connections and investment of energy into healthy, adult connections and friendships is worth it.

Take One Step into the Room

I recently attended my thirty-year high school reunion. By myself. With an injured dog at home, Andrew stayed behind and sent me on my way to see friends and find myself in the town that raised me. There I sat, in a parked car, entertaining the same thoughts I had when I was seventeen: *Please. Oh please! Please may I know someone here. Please may someone recognize me. PLEASE.* With two deep breaths, I grabbed my keys, and headed in. There, in the parking lot was a friend screaming, "Yes! Thank goodness you are here. I know someone!" She was quickly followed by my fourth-grade friend racing across the parking lot to swing into a hug as we reminisced about horror movies and our first boy-girl party. As you might guess, the evening flowed from there. It was totally cool to say, "Do I know you?" I made a few business connections (because we had dropped all pretense and realized a few of us are in a similar circle), got plenty of inspiration, and reconnected with me. At home. With friends from a lifetime ago. Friends who are cool with me being me. By taking that first step out of the car, I got in the game. And that's all I am inviting you to do. Right now.

To get (and keep) great clients, you must be willing to speak to them.

Sounds obvious, right? Yet, it seems to be the biggest hurdle when you finally decide you need to get out there and find yourself a client. While you have conversations every single day with colleagues and clients about substantive issues, the nuances in the law, or even firm politics, engaging in the ritual of client development (or worse yet, idle chit-chat) seems like pure torture. Talking to someone about sending you business conjures images of slimy salesmen in polyester suits, chewing gum, and calling you, "ma'am."

It gets more off-putting the longer you stay out of the game; and let's face it, you've been working way too hard to even know what the game looks like anymore. You studied hard in college to get into a good law school. Once there, you spent excruciatingly long hours buried in books, prepping for exams made to feel make-it or break-it. You got your first job and started proving yourself by working hard. You showed up early and stayed late; you answered the calls; you jumped into the projects, no matter the size—talking only to your colleagues, the walls of the file room, and the delivery driver handing you dinner. But there I go repeating myself.

Somewhere along this path, you stopped having real conversations. Family conversations became all about the logistics. Work conversations began to sound like a task list. You stopped intentionally getting to know other people, unless you're lucky enough to be invited to the wine-and-dine dinners . . . and then you talk to the person seated on either side of you. You lost connections from prior jobs and law school. You forgot to keep up with those that used to matter to you. At this point, you're not even sure friendships are a thing you get to have with the career you've chosen.

Turns out, hard work isn't the only skill set you need to get where you want to go. Namely, having a client roster filled with people and companies you like, who value your skills, and who aren't looking to wring every ounce out of you to get their dollar's worth.

When you stop looking around and meeting people, you get more complacent about putting yourself out there. It feels like you must be the only awkward one in the room every time you are asked to show up someplace new, find your way in a large networking event, show up for the firm retreat, or even grab coffee or lunch with a long-lost friend. You are positive everyone else has it together, and you might sound like the bumbling fool in the room.

So, you do what any self-respecting person would do. You stay away from that shit. Avoid it like the hot plague. This is only exacerbating the problem of getting over the hurdle of putting yourself out there.

As you might imagine, you need to get out of this rut. To do this, you must address the seriously crappy advice that is floating around about "networking" and conversations in general. Again, stop thinking about it as networking, and focus on relationship building. When you set aside images of racing to awful gatherings, you can let go of the stress of "being out there," and focus on building connections and conversations that lead to relationships.

Some other lousy stories that may be standing in your way . . .

1. You are either born a networker or not. False.

2. The gold only goes to the extroverts. Total rubbish.

3. Get out there and shake hands. Worst. Advice. Ever.

4. Sprinkle your business card around like confetti. (All I can think of is this one would hurt when they land.)

5. "Like" everyone's posts on LinkedIn so they know you care. (FYI lurking on social media doesn't check the real conversation column.)

Bad advice aside, you need to remember that this is both an art and a science, a skill and a practice. It's something you engage in, are consistent with, and pay attention to, so you can finally find the magic combination that is your personal recipe for business-building, relationship-conquering success.

No Salespeople Allowed

The old-school mentality is that you need to get out there, shake hands, always willing to schmooze just a little more. Join the committees, volunteer in the community, and in general, be around. As it turns out, focusing on getting out there, being seen (for the sake of being seen), and being heard (so everyone knows your sales pitch) will only get you so far. Instead, we want people to know you, not be sold by you.

When you try to make yourself sound like the schmoozy guy down the hall, it falls flat and makes it look and feel like you don't belong. The images and weirdness are enough to keep the most extroverted at home and send those who hate this crap running for the nearest bathroom.

But if you can get into a conversation, no way will you sink yourself to the level of appearing cheap and slimy. This is when you must double back to owning your space and place. Knowing yourself and being yourself—that's what opens doors. Recognize that you are moving relationships along through a progression of conversations; it will make the difference in how this whole process feels, and your ultimate success in making it work for you.

You Have What It Takes

There is a myth floating out there that you must have specific strengths to be a rainmaker. (One client told me a story about the firm expert announcing you are either born to make it rain or you are not . . . leaving her to the conclusion that there was no way it would work for her.)

But there is nothing any of us is born with that makes us able to "make it rain." Building a book is equally available for extroverts and introverts. You have what it takes. When you use your strengths as a route to get into the conversations and be true to your approach, the energy will resonate with colleagues, clients, and referral partners. This is where you allow yourself to show up how you want to be seen. In the right place, where you are comfortable and present when invited to the table for the big discussions and strategy sessions.

Find What Works

The best way to get out there is to find the plan that works for you, rather than thinking there is only one right way to engage in conversations and network. While my "methodology" requires zero racing to meals and drinks, others thrive in this arena, which means you use them if you enjoy them. The key is to find a way to network and engage in conversations that works for you.

Ask yourself to consider whether you would rather:

- pick up the phone for a great conversation.
- send an email sharing a hilarious video or fascinating article.
- grab a drink.
- enjoy a long meal with friends.
- build a network through LinkedIn that you engage in frequently.
- organize an event that brings others together.

Now, rank these options from 1-5 (1 is no way, not happening; 5 is let me grab my coat and let's do this). I invite you to scribble some notes in the margins or jot down what you think might resonate. Ranking the above options is a good start to remembering what works for you, not what everyone else is suggesting.

Now that you have a better idea of where you feel most comfortable showing up, you must have a simple way to get into the conversation. No need for a full conversation strategy yet, just a couple topics that you know resonate (a.k.a. ditch the indemnification clause banter).

That's right. When you show up for conversations worried about looking put together and sounding intelligent, you tend to rely on what you think others want to hear. Since you have only talked to these clients on the phone about a case or a deal, you move to the comfortable conversation of summary judgements and indemnification clauses. Whether this is habit or comfort does not matter, but it is blocking you from building connections. Puffing up and trying to sound smart is like taking a metal armor and wrapping yourself in it. No one can get to know you, and no one wants to stand too close. It's a shield, but also the one thing standing in your way of great connections and conversations. (I may be repeating myself here, but that's OK because this concept is vital.)

Put it another way: no one wants to be a part of a discussion (away from the actual negotiating table) that solely nerds out on the law. This is the single fastest way to send everyone to the bar during the cocktail party. Walking up to a group and telling them the story of how you were able to figure out the clause needed a "which" rather than a "that" and how it was going to blow your clients' minds is seriously not going to drive the droves of clients you are wishing for your way. This banter is typically a cover for wanting to avoid small talk or hoping to sound smart. And it doesn't land.

As indicated previously, potential clients want you to relate to the ordinary moments in life. People are interested in the human side of humanity. They want to exchange recipes and go for walks. They want to find the next show worth watching and learn about the best math tutoring service on the market. They want to reminisce about the lockdown days of the pandemic and even inch toward religion, politics, or money (depending on your circles and the context). Staying relevant means paying attention to current events and being at least somewhat aware of pop culture (or willing to own how out of touch you are, which is often my strategy).

This is where relationships are born: in your ability to join in daily conversations that are engaging, and highly effective, hinged on your ability to read the tone and tenor of the room. In fact, I have bonded more over my chicken soup and my mother's legendary brisket recipe than anything else. (If you want either, send me a note and it will be on the way: deb@debfeder.com.)

Activity:

For now, think about what you want to talk about sitting around the fire pit with a group of good friends. Make a list of everything that comes up. Then think about the last time you had a great laugh (not at your own failure to walk into the room) at a networking event: What were you talking about? Finally, think about the random stuff that always seems to come up when you grab lunch, or are stuck on a flight with a colleague. My favorite was exchanging stories about how we explain "life" to teens when I was stuck in O'Hare airport with a group of colleagues. I have never laughed so hard; and holy mackerel did those life lessons resonate. Let's just say, there were many different approaches.

Now go read what you included on this list. Circle the ones that you think are appropriate. Scratch off the ones that shouldn't make it to the cocktail party.

Star the ones you have seen others talking about on LinkedIn or in industry magazines. Finally, highlight what you could chat about all day long.

One more thing. Go back to your timeline. Think about one time you had a great client conversation, or a discussion that pops out in your mind. Mark it on the timeline. Again, it's part of what you bring to the table, and needs to be remembered.

Make the First Move

Is it just me or do nightmares of wanting to be included in the "cool kids club" still haunt you? (To think, this was before social media!) In middle school, you wanted to sit at the lunch table with those kids but didn't know if it was an invite-only thing, so you sat at a nearby table, hoping to catch someone's eye and have them wave you over. You waited and waited, awkwardly glancing over in your not-subtle teen way, until one day, while you were talking to one of those kids, they asked why you never sat with them at lunch. You didn't know whether to laugh or cry for all the time wasted thinking they would ask you first. Nonetheless, you gladly grabbed your lunch and joined them the next day, content that they'd made the first move. (Totally cool if I am going to be the only one to talk about wanting to meet or sit with or go out with someone in middle school. I can own this for all of us.)

Sadly, middle school social dynamics ends up being the training ground for professional practice and relationship-building. What you didn't know way back then (and remains true today), no one really feels like they belong; everyone wants to be invited by someone else.

Way too often, you get stuck not knowing where to start, or where you belong. Afraid of rejection or feeling awkward, you think the power center holds the cards. Until you figure out how to get the ball rolling, you are going to always be sitting at the table next to the great clients, waiting for them to nod your direction. When you wait to be invited, you are playing by someone else's rules. When you make the first move, the way it happens, the approach, and the results often sit squarely with you.

Building a book doesn't require you to start with conversations, seventh-grade style or otherwise, but at some point, they are going to become necessary.

Rest assured, there are plenty of ways to make the first move that work for everyone, no matter whether you thrive in the limelight, or would rather stick to staying home with a book and conducting your practice remotely. There's a way for you to get in the game.

Play It Out

When clients first call me, this is often the spot they want to figure out. They want to "get out there" and bring in clients, without having a clue where to begin. They have been invited to parties, formal pitches, conferences, and seminars, with little or nothing to show for it in terms of actual new clients. This is when you have been playing the long game, waiting for others to make introductions, which plays out in a few not-so-awesome ways:

1. You wait for the call to come that everyone is meeting up and they would like you to join them. That's the loooong game.

2. You wait until that conference coming up in the fall. Certain you will run into them there. That's where you will warm them up to the conversation. Hmm . . . hope they show up. These days, that's a fifty-fifty proposition at best.

3. You get to that conference to find that your buddy at the rival firm has already invited a group to dinner. You set out to enjoy room service, convincing yourself that this is how you would have wanted the night to end, so whatevs.

4. You get to that dinner and sit next to the clients, hoping for just the right moment to bring up the idea you would like to learn more about. Waiting to jump in, you end up following along the ring leader's crazy conversation, then walk away wondering the appropriate timeframe for following up, so you don't look like a stalker.

There's one more option. Put yourself in the driver's seat. Instead of obsessing about being called out of the blue, or cornering one target client at some conference, spread out the effort. The process is not a numbers game, but one based on relationships, testing, and tweaking in groups of three to five as you go.

Consider the story of a client we'll call Matilda. Matilda came to me wanting a book of business. She was a little flipped out about where to start, so we took a couple of deep breaths together and decided we needed a starting point: first, get in the game; second, find out what Matilda noticed from some easy, no-pressure conversations.

Matilda started with about five people she had met recently at conferences and a few networking events. She had business cards and had promised to follow up. Someday. And that day was now.

Deciding there was relatively little to lose, she sent the "circling back" emails to each of the individuals, reconnecting them to the prior conversation they had when running into each other. Checking in to see if they wanted to connect, grab a coffee, or jump on the phone (depending on where they were geographically). She went in with extremely low expectations.

What happened flipped her mindset on a dime. Each of them was excited to reconnect, have a longer conversation, and talk about mutual projects and ideas that they were building out.

Some have turned into referrals, others into business. Each was an opportunity that wouldn't have happened if she had pitched those business cards in the trash.

Matilda's next instinct. Umm . . . panic! Not expecting them to bite, she assumed this was a useless exercise; she was just humoring me. Not so much.

After deep breaths and a smidge of strategy, she was ready to head to the first lunch. She picked casual venues. Nothing fancy. Nothing shouting "long-term commitment" from the rafters. The conversations came naturally. Because she put it out there with that tone. There was no need for a pitch, but some asked for her to send over details of her work. Others wanted to know if they could invite her to speak or connect her with colleagues. Not panicking, Matilda was open to seeing the opportunity right in front of her face. Because it happened, one after another. How do I know? I got the call after each one. We celebrated (OK, we legit turned cartwheels to be specific), and then got to work seeing the smallest of next steps. Which is often just a deep breath—no panic or racing to chase after them. Just being you.

Matilda is now in the position to figure out which clients resonate, and which relationships aren't Ideal. She is giving back to the relationships, making introductions, and enjoying the process of building this career. Her own way. And she's having fun in the process. Because fun is contagious. So is loving what you do. And knowing Matilda, fun and loving what you do exudes from her in every moment of these conversations.

A Word on Being a Creepster

Now, you still might be thinking, "I need to find a way to get to that coffee with the bigwig client I'm after. So, I better start stalking." As it turns out, there are professional equivalents to the half-stalking methods of middle school that are a sad attempt to get the attention of the cool kids (now known as clients). None of these are good. In fact, they're creepy AF.

1. Cocktail party stalking. You follow around that one contact you have been dying to get in front of for years, the one *finally* at the same networking event. Armed with a drink, business card, and firm handshake, you stake out the high-top table right next to your target. You laugh when the group laughs, hoping they invite you to join in. Not sure how long to stand around, you end up sipping the end of the bottom of the drink for way too long, finally grabbing your phone to give you something to look at.

2. The instant messenger intro with a pitch for business. It reads something like, "Hey, Deb, I noticed we both went to Michigan undergrad and Iowa law. My work is focused on helping lawyers streamline their emails with autoreplies. Pretty sure I could be useful to your clients.

Want to connect soon?" Followed every two days with something like, "Hey, Deb, haven't heard from you, still interested?" This speaks for itself. Please, just don't.

3. The more subtle LinkedIn connection. You hope this sparks a future conversation, at least recognition of your name. This is all good until you start popping up on their posts every single day, friending everyone they know, and commenting on everything with the likes of, "You are so wise; what a great perspective you and your company have." Adding value requires a more subtle approach to sharing your excellence (and presence).

4. Asking for an introduction from the mutual connection that you met once or twice. While this has the possibility of being successful, you are also waiting for others to remember to make the introduction and hoping they do it in a way that puts you in the best light.

5. Standing around with a cigarette holder in your hand (insert 1950s prop) in the hopes of being seen, appearing memorable and well-prepared for this moment in the sun. The modern approach to this is putting out your thought leadership pieces and name-dropping everyone who you have ever brushed elbows with. Oh, you've heard the lousy advice from experts that sounds something like:

> *Be patient. Share your expertise. Make sure your name is out there. When they need you, they will remember they saw your name. One day. You will see. They will call.*

My thoughts on this approach are well documented, but just in case you are not 100% clear:

> *Lord. This is less effective than speed dating or hoping the ideal client with the multi-million-dollar book finds you through a pay-per-click ad on the internet.*

While all these methods seem viable on the surface, the awkward nature to all of them, and less direct method of getting into the conversation, leaves a whole lot to be desired.

I am going to be honest with you. Clients are waiting to be invited to talk to you just as much as you are waiting for them to call. This waiting is a terrible game of chicken that no one will win. You know who gets the conversation: the brave soul willing to make the first move.

Cool Ways to Make the First Move

Now, it would not be cool if I refrained from telling you some legit ways to make the first move. On the surface, some of these may not look as effective as bugging a target client on LinkedIn day in and day out, but trust me when I say this is the way to the promised land.

1. Create a think tank. While these have many forms, bringing together people who are all working in a similar space, from different angles, to bounce ideas, share trends, and get to know each other is often underappreciated and underutilized. Because these are the very people who are going to know the Ideals you want to serve and will connect you to them. Because they know, like, and trust you. That's how relationships work.

   Example: Women Lawyers' Lunch. Every month women lawyers gather to meet, eat a virtual lunch, network, and talk about the big topics. They represent different types of clients; they're eager to collaborate, learn from each other, and influence the next generation of women in law. Super fun, super effective. And a place to know you can meet others at zero barrier to entry. Also, low risk and easy to implement within your firms, clients, and friends.[11]

2. Ask for the conversation. This works particularly well with anyone other than a cold call. Start with someone who knows you and is willingly to share ideas (someone from your think tank, for example); start practicing your curious conversations by picking just one topic you want to learn about. Narrow down what you are looking to create, study, and understand. Experts typi-

[11] Want to join? Open to all women lawyers. Just send me a note to get on the list.

cally love sharing their expertise, so allow them to share wisdom with you. This becomes particularly valuable when you start comparing conversations with different players within the same field. When the perspectives can shed a little light on an area you are also building your expertise in, and becoming known for, this is market research in the moment. These conversations tend to create a nice jumping point to gather folks for the think tank. (See how it all loops together?)

Example: A great way to pivot from casual, friendly banter into a business focus is by asking a simple question: "While we are talking, I am wondering what you think about [insert something that intersects their work, your expertise, approach, or methodology]?" or "What are you hearing everyone say about [insert current topic or emerging issue]?" or "What do you wish [outside counsel, your colleagues, the deal teams] would understand before calling you?" These questions casually pivot into a broader conversation, allowing you to ask for more details. While my clients know I love a solid, three question strategy, this is the start. And exactly where you need to be to start building a new trust bucket with clients (both current and potential).

3. Reach out to others when you're around. These others might be current clients, referral sources, experts in your field, or in an adjacent industry. Again, keep it

casual, not a big deal. Before heading out, let others know that you will be around, and you would love to get together. If it works on the schedule, take a few minutes for coffee, and learn about what's new in their world.

Example: Heading to a city with time to spare for a quick coffee? Send an email and check if schedules can match to make it happen. If nothing else, you can use this as an opportunity to speak to them more than the casual "hello" or LinkedIn post. Asking for recommendations on the city is a good ice breaker, and way to jump start a conversation at the same time. Bonus points if you can gather a few people together.

Be That Person

We all know the house that is always willing to have the parties and invite everyone over. They make the first move. Invite everyone. Put it out there. They pick the menu and the movie. They control the situation. When it comes to getting and keeping clients, you can be that person, too. You can be *the* house.

Being the person that starts it all in a relationship is a power play. Be that person. The one who lets everyone know the conference is coming and you are putting together a group for coffee, lunch, cocktails, dinner . . . everyone appreciates the person who plans. Crowd source something low key and make it happen.

Tip: tacos and blue jeans over the formal sit-down wine dinner. Find a cool place and enjoy being the coordinator of the guest list and the fun.

Activity:

Pick a couple of colleagues from law school—ones you run into from time to time or someone with whom you mean to reconnect. Next to each name decide whether you would like to invite them out, catch up over a call, or introduce them to someone else. Send a short email to find out what works for them.

Don't panic. Don't overthink it. Just reach out. Keep it casual.

At this point, you are building your muscle of being the one to make the first move. And let me be the first one to tell you how incredibly proud I am that you went ahead and hit "send" on those emails. We'll work on what to say and how to handle it next. I promise.

Curiosity Leads to Clients

Lawyers are taught to be smart. Even in the moments where we feel incredibly stupid, we'll talk. We'll share. We'll keep talking, until somehow, we spot a spark of recognition in the listener's eye that's interpreted as resonating. Then, we take a deep breath and pause.

Turns out, this is the wrong strategy for letting your smarts shine through. On the flip side, a great way to go about it is to join a conversation through the lens of curiosity. When you let your insightful questions give a glimpse of your smarts, it allows the conversation to be all about them.

Why? Because people like to share their opinions. They also like to be considered the expert. When you give an Ideal the respect of being viewed in both lights, your smarts do not threaten to outshine their experience. You are joining them on even ground. Making the case for a very nice reciprocal relationship. One that works for you both.

I love my in-laws, yet when I first met them, they interviewed me as if I'd applied for a million-dollar-a-year job. I can still remember the restaurant, the table, and the drive with my now-husband on the way there. At that table, my father-in-law took the lead. He allowed me two sips of water before he launched into a long line of questions. An hour later, the man knew everything there was to know about my family, my days at Michigan, and my practice. He might have taken a health history as well, but I've thankfully blocked that out. (I simply tried to rapid fire my responses back, like good legal training had prepped me.) Finally satisfied, he simply nodded and told me he thought his son was going to turn out OK, which I took to mean I'd passed the test. Thinking back, I laugh because I now recognize he wasn't just concerned with my merits, but wanted to make sure his son made a good decision and looked good to me, too. Questions can cover so many jobs.

Now, while I certainly don't advocate sitting down with an Ideal and interrogating them with a bare light bulb overhead, I am a big believer in guiding the conversation from Point A to Point B by asking great questions.

For starters, this puts you in the driver's seat.

If you've ever done any sales training, you understand that the minute the client is in control of the questions, you have lost control of the direction of the conversation. You will suddenly find yourself in the defensive mode, worried about the answer and sounding awkwardly perfect. But this is not about grabbing a sale. You are focused on building a relationship, and allowing a client to know what you do, without whipping that pitch out of your pocket.

Healthy Client Relationships Are Meant to Be Reciprocal

Let's step back for one quick second and examine how good working relationships work. Just like every contract requires consideration that is commiserate with the work and value being provided, the same applies to the actual underlying attorney-client relationship for it to be a healthy, productive one. When you forget this one point, imbalance occurs, and you start fighting for every inch of ground, right from the start.

Here are a few ways you voluntarily give up your power right from the start. I've talked about one of them before, but it bears a reminder.

1. Drop your rates. You believe clients won't be willing to pay that rate—that you're not worthy, so you lower it before they even ask. Then, when your numbers don't add up, you blame them.

2. Tell them you are always available. Setting the standard that they call the timing shots, no matter what, you hand over a permission slip to call anytime. When they use

it, you're pissed.

3. Being the working partner for a client. You know, the one who will always take care of everything, especially while senior partner is on vacation every summer for six weeks. It might seem like a good idea, but the list of complications this comes with could fill its own library.

When you give up power, you walk into the relationship with an edge, and everything feels lopsided. Believe it or not, clients can sense this. They can feel you grumbling on the other end of the unanswered phone. They get when they are not your top priority, when their work is shoved to the bottom, and when you aren't getting it.

They also assume you are being straight when you offer over-the-top options and make things cheaper and easier for them right from the start. It's not their fault when they take advantage of it. On top of all this, it is extremely hard to regulate the power imbalance once you start off on the wrong foot. It can only happen over time and requires you to double down on showing up and being seen, but when you do, the trust equation falls in your favor, as the trusted advisor who can be relied on by the client at all turns.

It's also important to note that while you are out there looking for something better, the clients are doing the same. More often than you'd guess, the "better" may simply be equalizing the power and relationship dynamics with the great clients already around you, the very people who could be sending you a lot more work. Again, this is a lesson on relationships based on trust.

Before you completely dismiss me, you are correct that, at the end of the day, the client must decide to pick you for the case, the project, or the deal. You are right that the client can move the work at a moment's notice. By focusing on that one transactional point in the relationship, however, you miss all the opportunity. If you persist in operating as if every client deserves to be on your roster when they don't, that every client is a perfect fit for you when they're not, you're missing the point.

With that, it's time to figure out how to turn the conversations you have jump-started into a client generation machine. But first, let's make sure we're on the same page and review where you are in the conversation strategy:

1. You have decided to ditch the complaining and waiting for this career to work out on its own.

2. You have brushed off your relationships and started reaching out. Which has been OK.

3. You have then moved into the starter conversations. Again, not terrible.

4. Now . . . you want them to call you, hire you, and send you the first great project.

The Conversation Progression

The following is the progression of how you move conversations from one phase to another, moving to the right moment where you can ask for work, or be available for the right opportunities. There is no timing requirement at any given stage; as a matter of fact, you often move back and forth along this progression. If you move too fast to the aggressive end point (the "Nice to meet you, can I have your business" kind of way), you will miss the opportunity to lay the foundation, so the ending can work out in your favor.

This is where you realize you need to ignore the lousy advice that offers up a formula for how long you stay at each stage in a client lunch. Did you know that some say when you're at the table, you should engage only in small talk until you place your order? Once the food arrives, you can pivot to more serious matters. I'm not sure what happens over dessert—maybe that's where you ask for a hefty retainer check.

Seriously, though, if this is not weird, I don't know what is. What ever happened to the natural ability to be aware of the conversation and go with the flow? Then guiding the conversation with some serious Jedi mind tricks.

Oh, so you want those Jedi tricks, do you?

1. Start with small talk. This is all about building rapport, catching up, and setting the groundwork for just being human in the conversation. There is so much value here. Understanding how to settle into the banter and use it to tighten the connections cannot be understated or undervalued.

2. Pivot and learn. Once everyone has taken a deep breath and the conversation opens (there is a moment this happens), your job is to be interested in their perspective. This is merely the advanced class of being interested in them. At this point, ask something along the lines of, "While we are talking, I am curious about your thoughts on ______________."

   Now, you carefully craft what goes into that blank. It's about more than asking a good question (another step way too many get wrong); it's a way to open the dialogue. And allow yourself to sit back, enjoy your sandwich, and listen.

3. Validate and understand. While you listen, pay attention to the actual words being spoken. Seems simple, right? Yet, it is the one thing everyone messes up. You're particularly prone to error because you've perfected the craft of synthesizing information in law school,

through years of weeding through tedious conversations about the law, then quickly absorbing information and translating it into your own words. But the client doesn't care about your interpretation of what they're saying (no matter how smart it sounds). They just care about what they're saying and how they're saying it.

A note about botching this: when you twist and interpret clients' words, or worse yet talk over them, there is a high likelihood you instill doubt in their minds. Assuming you weren't listening, they jump to the all-too-often-accurate assumption that you are simply one more lawyer who wants to appear savvy.

Here's the thing: if they didn't think you were at least a smidge smart, they wouldn't be at lunch (or anywhere else, for that matter) with you. Lots of people are smart. But very few people care enough to ask awesome questions, then hold back and listen. You want to be one of the very few.

4. Advance the work. This part seems to be the most daunting for everyone, yet when the first three steps are done well, the rest takes care of itself.

   When you listen to clients and learn, you are in the position to offer the solutions they are looking for. (Remember, you asked them about what they need, are worried about, want to have fixed, or are seeking to understand.) You have put yourself in the position as the most valuable outside, trusted resource they have—one that they want to have on their team.

Hold back the urge to pull the pitch out to ensure they hear it before you go. If you really must go there, keep it steady and simple: "Hey, the next time you have a project like _______ on your desk, I would love to talk about it," works. Even better, "if you would like us to sit down and strategize about ____________, just let me know, we are happy to put the resources you need together."[12]

5. Follow up. Too often, you walk away from the conversation, moment, or opportunity and unsure what happens next. This is where you spend a lot of time getting strategic about the timing of the follow-up and next steps.

   First, if you promised to be working on something, introducing them, or putting their big thoughts into action, you better get started and not forget. This falls into the sooner rather than later category. Your follow-through right here is how they will judge your interpretation of responsiveness.

---

[12] Please, please, please remember to make sure the exact words you use sound like you, rather than me.

Similarly, if the meeting was kind of a pitch and they mentioned sending you work, follow up within twenty-four hours after the discussion. Recognize they mentioned this and let them know you are available to discuss the next steps. Better yet? Before you walk away, ask them how they would like you to follow up. Then, follow their direction.

Next, if there was a casual mention of a follow-up—to continue the discussion or expand the conversation to include others—it should happen within three to five days. Again, this is more for you not to drop the ball than to hurry them. This follow up can be as simple as an appreciation for their thoughts and a "looking forward to us getting the chance to regroup and continue the conversation." You might even ask them to throw out times that work to meet in the next few weeks (or whatever is appropriate based on the discussion).

But if you simply had a good conversation (the most common occurrence), put them on your follow-up list. Then, every month or so, circle back, share something of interest with them, or simply touch base. While there is a lot more to the connection strategy here, the key is this: don't lose track of whom you've talked to, and remember to remember them.

Why is the curious conversation progression so wickedly effective? Because it blends the best of all worlds . . .

1. It gives you a job. Hate joining a conversation? Wish

you could hide in the corner and just get work and be good? I get it. But, since you must talk to the clients to get them to hire you, you might as well keep your busy brain occupied with an actual task, rather than letting worry overtake rational thoughts.

2. It allows you to show up as a professional without putting it on your name badge. Asking great questions requires you to have the knowledge and information to create the right scenario for your expertise to shine through. The easy questions—"tell me about your work," or worse yet, "how's work"—don't tell you a thing. Asking a strategic question lets your smarts shine through.

3. It lets you tap into your law school researcher skills. When done well, you can gather data from the conversations you engage in with even three to five people. When you start understanding the commonalities in how they answer the same questions, you'll start to see trends; you can create content that addresses those issues; you can focus your practice in such a way that it resonates with more than one client. Suddenly, you have the base of a book of business.

Example: In response to the COVID kerfuffle of everyone being sent home, law firms, consultants, and accounting firms start pumping out 100+ page guides on COVID. The purpose was to respond to the panic ensuing both internally and externally by doing what experts do best: throw man hours and words at the problem to position the firm as the go-to experts. A rational fear response that missed the mark.

Chock-full of data, all guides had two things in common: one, a picture of a germ on the front that looked remarkably like my grandmother's sponge; two, they primarily ended up in the trash bin (either electronically, or in those new home offices).

What if, instead of throwing a thousand man-hours and countless marketing professionals at a rush project, you picked up the phone and called three to five Ideals (current or prospective) affected by the crisis. Without sugar-coating things, you agree there is nothing you can do about a pandemic—but you ask what you can do to make sure everything is running as well as possible the following Monday. These Ideals mention the desire for a simple checklist. You continue these calls and keep hearing the same request.

So, you take your conversation and put it into action:

1. You do not create a guide. You create a checklist. This sends the message that you pay attention.

2. You do not tell the client they are wrong, that they need more. You give them what they are asking for right now and know that you will be the resource when they need the full-on guide.

3. You do recognize that there is a request for simplicity and the checklist must have certain features.

4. You spend a few hours creating it, then send it over asking for them to weigh in and share anything else they might find useful.

5. You freely hand out the checklist, using it as a credibility builder. Because at the end of the day this is building the trust platform to hire you. Believe in you. And want you hired to represent them.

6. You can use it for content on LinkedIn, blogs, or video. You can talk about why a checklist is necessary, and not a guide. You can also talk about why a checklist is only the first step, thereby opening the opportunity to expand the discussion. (While we might argue about the line between work product and thought leadership, this investment of time and dollars is far less than the massive investment in creating blogs, reports, and guides that are flying under the radar and ending up in the shredder.)

7. When you expand the discussion, Ideals will hone in on you because you're right there in the middle of a conversation they're heavily invested in.

One quick warning: you must be willing to listen and not solve in the moment of those conversations. This means you literally must keep your lips zipped shut. You can be conversational, but don't try to Band-Aid the problem they are talking about. You cannot dismiss them or argue with them on why they are short-sighted or wrong. This comes off as posturing, and you look like one more talking head that they are sick of hearing from.

When you are willing to listen and intentionally hear what someone is saying, you will be surprised. Now, pause that brain of yours that wants to insist you've been doing this a long time, you know what your clients want and need. I get that, so have all my clients; yet over and over this plan works because you finally hear what the clients have been wanting you to get, which you seem to gloss over in favor of cranking out work product.

When you pay attention to how the conversation unfolds, you may realize that insisting on bringing the clients in for wine dinners and fancy-schmancy events is just an annoyance in their schedules; their big worry is trying to find the perfect teacher gift. (Tip: this is often discovered in the small-talk portion of our conversations.)

It might mean they need to share their worries about industry trends and need someone to hear them out—to bounce ideas about what's next for them, the department, or the deals sitting in the queue.

I don't know what you will find out, but when you start listening, you will start to hear common words and themes—

and the verbiage will help you resonate with your clients right from the start.

The faster you can help those synapses see the connection between your work and what they need, the better off you are. Which means you and your work need to resonate with Ideals, build a stronger foundation on which to trust you and your expertise, and make your opinions worth having at the table. And no shiny pitch packet can do this as well as asking super simple, strategic questions. Not even close.

Test, Trial, Tweak

I am a great cook. Yet, most of my well-loved meals have gone through some serious testing—trying a new recipe, making my family try it, and tweaking the recipe repeatedly until it's close to perfection. Conversations and client relationships require the same amount of testing.

This process allows you to figure out if your efforts to build client relationships via networking and conversations are working or not. Let's be honest, how do you know if you're attracting the right kind of people with your newfound approach? If you are waiting until the book numbers look incredible on the annual partner report that has the envy of your colleagues, you are going to miss the mark completely.

You know the old school mentality of pitch, wait, pray; get yourself out there and someday the right clients will call; share your ideas on LinkedIn, people will remember your name; get on panels, and they will line up to hire you?

All these "strategies" are banked on the idea that building a legal career is a long game. Plant the seeds today and wait to see which ones bloom in the years to come. (No one ever asks what kinds of seeds you've bothered to plant, but hey, whatever.)

With all due respect . . . this is a terrible idea.

When you play a long game, you can't determine which of your efforts are working, which are missing the mark. It also acts as an excuse to hold back or not try at all, since the "long game" has no deadline.

Firms are filled with annual traditions of putting together practice plans that often include brushing off numbers and client names once a year, in the hope that no one notices you have no clue how it will all work. Not to mention the big fat assumption that the clients the year before stuck around. Until you figure out a better way to quell the justifiable anxiety, you are going to stick with pitch, wait, pray, and keep your fingers crossed that something new pulls through one of these days and makes that annual meeting a little easier. Surprise, *a $1mm+ client just fell from the sky!*

To better gauge, you need to pace the progression in a way that allows you to try, test, and tweak your networking-for-clients engagement quickly, to determine which efforts are in fact worth it, and which are not. You don't have time to waste on useless exercises for years to come.

Be the Researcher

Start with simple, curious conversations. No begging for work or awkward off-the-cuff pitches. No sales. Simply engage with clients, colleagues, referral partners to learn more about who you put into the Ideal bucket for right this minute. Keep your questions simple and consistent; use that inquisitive muscle that got you through law school to start gathering data (the stuff everyone else is looking over and missing out on).

Example: A client of mine (let's call him Eric) engaged in fourteen curious conversations in the first month of working with me. His work was all about the tech and the invaluable analysis it could provide, with many industry players competing for the same clients. Yet, the efforts to land the clients and showcase the amazing tech was falling flat, repeatedly. Since Eric wanted to grow his book, the first task was to find out what these clients, the ones who needed the tech to manage their big client projects, cared about. Diving into researcher mode, Eric was stunned to find the clients he talked to weren't all that interested in the technology (which was no surprise to me). What clients cared about was getting the results, the data, and making sure the tech wasn't slowing the rest of their analysis and case strategy down.

The core issue was timing. Yet, no one was discussing it, until Eric had these conversations and changed the focus. When the focus turned to timing—what it could be; why it isn't always that important—it opened relationships and created trust, up front. That is the power of being OK with not knowing everything.

Now, you might be worried that asking such questions, or any questions for that matter, will make you look incompetent. Yet, the contrary is true (so long as you are asking good questions). Those who do this and listen, rise above the lot and shine. Others recognize the commitment and the dedication to being at the table, rather than just being part of the crowd shouting to the wind. You may assume that, armed with this information, the next step is to ask for the business. But think bigger. Use your newfound insights to gain trust, attract other clients, and establish your expertise (and, most likely, land the client).

Share the Info Wisely

When you use the language and details learned from conversations, LinkedIn, webinars, blogs, podcasts, and articles become effective. Gather the perspective and ideas of your Ideals, referral partners, and colleagues, and your words will resonate (even if you disagree with their analysis). You won't simply catch a fish with your words, you will make them happy to be in your net, and bring in several others along for the ride.

Of course, when you use the information you've gathered, it's important to know what those perfect clients are looking for—not what you assume they care about. Consider this the bait.

When your work resonates and you have already shown yourself capable of being interested (rather than trying to be the interesting one), your clients, colleagues, and referral partners want you at the table. Every time. They want to know what you know. They want to hear your perspective. They know you are willing to work with them to find answers, and get the work done. Your job? Show up for the conversations.

Show Up How You Want to Be Seen

Show up as the professional you want to be. This is the whole "do good work and be responsive" thing, where you choose to be excellent. For example, choose to have a voicemail that can accept messages; meet (or beat) deadlines (versus consistently pushing them back). Trust me. They notice. They talk about it. And if the opportunity comes their way, they will look around. Often the key to getting clients to stick around is right at this stage.

To recap:

1. Start and stay with rapport until it feels comfortable and appropriate to move into a deeper conversation.

2. Pivot your discussion to inquire about something that falls within a mutual interest. Show up curious and gather data. Ask strategic questions to get into the conversation.

3. Pay attention to what you learn from the conversation. Know what resonates with your audience (the clients and referral partners). Notice themes. Test your assumptions.

4. Share content and ideas based on these conversations, so your clients and those you haven't met yet, think you're talking right to them.

5. Your work, professionalism, and decision to be excellent shine through in all you do.

Again, the cool thing about this approach is you can bounce around. You can focus on different areas, depending on whether you are in ramp-up or ramp-down mode—and where your clients need you to be. Whether slammed and need to double down on responsiveness, or you need to jump into conversations to start generating new work, know how to work the system. It's where the magic happens.

Step 3:

Engage in 30 Conversations in 30 Days

Engage in 30 Conversations in 30 Days

Now that you've spent all this time gearing up for great conversations, it's time to put what you learned into practice. You'll find thirty conversations, below. For the first month, your mission is to give each one a try. See what happens; then, make a new plan to try them again in month two. To make it easy, the Guide has a checklist for you to mark off each time you complete a conversation. This is a great place to find an accountability partner and check in frequently to share how the conversations are landing and which ones you are committing to complete next.

Start with Those You Know

Consider this the warm-up to bigger conversations. Practice connecting and engaging in simple conversations with those already around you. As discussed, often the Ideals, and ideal projects, are already sitting right next to you, waiting for you to pay attention.

Conversation #1: Say Hello

While this may seem too simplistic on face value, it really is the very best conversation starter out there. Stuck in routines, it's easy to lose track of those you see every day. So, pause for a moment for the simple hello—to a work colleague, client, or someone you consistently see around the neighborhood or at the grocery store. If it's someone you don't know well, it's perfectly appropriate to give them your name and ask for a reminder of their name. Above all, enjoy the conversation.

Conversation #2: Catch Up with a Colleague

You work with people. Whether you are in an AmLaw 100 firm, or launched your own boutique practice, you are surrounded by people who support you and your work. Pause to have a conversation with these individuals. It does three things: one, gives you practice; two, builds camaraderie with those around you; and three, builds trust. Be curious about what they are working on, who else they work with, and what they are noticing. Who knows? You just might learn something (often they've been waiting for the moment to tell you about an idea or ask that question). For this one, stay curious and engaged.

Conversation #3: Catch Up with Your Old Boss or Colleague

Find someone you used to work with—someone from a prior position, or that first internship—and catch up. What's transpired since you last talked? What's new? What's the same? These are the people who watched you "grow up" in your work. They were around for your bloopers and big wins. Catching up should feel easy and light. A helpful note: focus on touching base with healthy work relationships from the past.

Conversation #4: Catch Up with Your Childhood Friend
Too often those who knew you before your career are often overlooked. But they are the ones who remember getting in trouble when you missed curfew or how your mother made fajitas on Tuesday nights. The stories are often memories. You need to catch up, find out what they are doing, and realize that although your lives may have grown in different directions, you have more in common than you think. These are great jump starters prior to a reunion or catching up after a hometown visit. Trust me, they are worth it!

Client Conversations

Once you've warmed up with those you know, it's time to focus on client conversations—the ones you must have, the ones you want to have, and the ones that are opportunities staring you in the face.

Conversation #5: The Touchbase
Sometimes you just need to check in. This one is simple. Send a quick email asking for a time to connect and catch up. What do they have going on? What are they working on? What are they stressed about? Remember to be a good listener. If you really give a hoot, you must pay attention. Bonus if you can find a way to help them afterward.

Conversation #6: The Celebration

When those around you hit a homerun, make sure to send a note of congratulations. Let them know what impresses you about the accomplishment and what you would love to learn more about. Hold back the urge to make this moment about you or compare it to you . . . this is their time to shine. Even if you were part of the "win," let them have the spotlight and enjoy being the guide that helped them make it happen.

Conversation #7: Learning Moments

Not everything goes as planned. Sometimes you must own the stuff that didn't play out quite the way it was intended. When you decide each step of the way to be a bit better next time, it makes you the expert people seek out. You develop this conversation by debriefing what went well and what wasn't a win with your clients (after a project ends or along the way, as appropriate). Be willing to listen and learn; it goes a long way in building trust. Celebrate what went well and make note of the changes for next time. Express your appreciation for the opportunity and start talking about what's next on the plate.

Conversation #8: The Project Update

This one can be positive or rehabilitative in nature, depending on what's going on with the project. When you are worried about the status of a project, either because it's been lingering too long on someone's desk (even your own), or because something seems off, get into a conversation with the client or colleagues involved. Send a quick note letting them know you have been reviewing the open items for ____________ and have a few questions. Ask for a call to get on the same page regarding ____________. Once you get this reset, don't waste it. Follow through and keep the project moving forward.

Conversation #9: Follow Up

If you had lunch, met for a meeting, or finished a project with someone, you need a follow-up. This is the easiest opportunity to continue the conversation—and the most missed. Continuing the conversation and moving it to the next stage is often where the ball is dropped. Keep this note simple; make sure to include anything you promised to deliver. If it's been way too long since you were supposed to touch base, remember to include a simple apology for the delay.

Conversation #10: The Lost Client

Do you have former clients with whom you haven't kept in touch, but you'd like to rekindle the relationship? Here are a few tips to get you started:

Spark a conversation by sending an email letting them know their name came up; you were remembering __________; or realized it has been way too long since you had the chance to connect. You would love an update on where they are and hope to connect soon. People love to reconnect. Especially when they had a relationship with you before. This often sparks a project or client relationship quickly because you remind them what's on their desk, and that you have been a trusted resource in the past.

Conversation #11: The Bill Is Actually Business Development

How many times have you dreaded having a conversation with a client about collecting on an invoice? Well, turn this conversation around and make it about strengthening the relationship (versus that awkward conversation about money and that billable hour). These conversations often happen during "collection season" at the end of the year, or when the client has a question about what's on the bill. Instead of avoiding them or pushing them off to an assistant or billing department, participate and use it as an opportunity to build rapport. Hear the question, discuss the work product, and make sure you have a common understanding. It creates a lot of trust for the work to come next. One caveat: you must know what the bill says and the work that was completed before you get into the conversation.

Conversation #12: Expand the Work

This is a work conversation. Progressing the relationship from one small project to being the trusted advisor means you need to get into the bigger projects and conversations with the Ideal. My approach is simple. Ask how they are handling the developments with [insert current hot topic] or what they are hearing others' reactions to [insert hot topic]. What do they have in place for the work that needs to get done? What do you need to work effectively? If you uncover something they don't have (but would serve them well)—something you could do—casually mention it . . . with the caveat you can talk about it another time. You are planting the seeds for future work.

For example, when I was in private practice, it would start with one simple project. I would always ask for guidelines, terms they like to use, or forms. When those weren't available (because they didn't have them), I would casually offer it up as something we could discuss someday to save them time and money going forward. This would often lead to an ask to go ahead and get started on that right away. Taking on the forms lets you be the trusted advisor going forward, without ever having to get pushy or weird.

Conversation #13: Introduce Others

This is a power move. Think about all the times you think someone should connect with someone else. Too often such thoughts pass in a moment, and you fail to follow through. Your challenge here is to get it done. Pick two people (go easy; don't pick your two biggest clients) and invite them to connect. The email should look something like this:

> Reva and Ruth,
>
> I hope you are both doing well. I wanted to introduce the two of you with the hopes that you can connect. Ruth, Reva makes an incredible macaroni and cheese. Reva, Ruth is known for her tuna sandwiches. I hope the two of you can connect and talk about making lunches.
> Have a great day!
> Deb

(P.S. Reva and Ruth were my grandmothers—and the mac and cheese was totally questionable.)

Conversation #14: Referral Partners Are the Keys to the Kingdom

When you get a chance to talk to others who are working with your clients, it's a powerful conversation. These might be financial advisors, investment bankers, insurers . . . anyone who is also involved in the work you do, just from a different angle. Knowing who else is talking with your Ideals, allows you to learn from others. This is an opportunity for curious conversations and practicing excellent listening skills. You want to know more about those they work with; when they are brought into the conversation; how they help. This, in turn, helps inform you of the conversations you need to be leading with your Ideals.

Working for the Business

If all goes according to plan, at some point, you must be ready to talk about yourself and your work—whether a formal pitch, or informal meeting where you are invited to share what you do to the powers-that-be. Prep for these and show up confident and ready!

Conversation #15: The Real Pre-Pitch Conversation

These are the real ones. The ones where you have been invited to share your experience and expertise for a particular type of work. There are many resources out there for prepping. But this is the conversation that leads up to it. When you are given the opportunity, don't just smile and say, "OK." Get curious. Find out if there are any areas or concerns that need to be included in your presentation and who will be involved. This allows you to start doing the prep work the right way. Listen to what you are being told (and what you aren't being told). Take a few minutes and think about what you need to feel confident you can bring the right information and team to the table. Have this list handy for when the opportunities come your way (and they will).

One note, if you are new to the pitch process, use this as an opportunity to talk with other lawyers you work with on how they prep and the questions they like answered up front. Use your curiosity as a learning moment, and chance to do some internal networking.

Conversation #16: Engage in Big Talk (a.k.a. Advocate for Yourself)

To walk into meetings feeling confident, you need to practice owning your own success. Think of a situation where you need to advocate for yourself, or even brag a bit about the results you achieved—big or small, and everything in between. Find a friend or colleague you trust and share the good news. Make sure to include your win and why it's significant for you. The key here? Don't diminish your win and don't make it bigger than it is. (You didn't solve world peace, and it isn't the equivalent of a good grade on a spelling test.)

For this one, send me an email (deb@debfeder.com) and let me know about the big win. (I love to celebrate with my clients; and I want you to understand how having a cheering section can give you the momentum needed to keep going for that next goal.) The only criteria: you recognize the win is important, and you want to share it!

The Networking Event

You know the scene: you walk in to find a buffet of amazing food, right next to a fully stocked bar; a crowd surrounds the gregarious guy, telling hilarious stories. You look around. Groups of two to four gather, talking amongst themselves. Since you were brave enough to get out of the car and walk in the door, you must decide what to do next. Once you have your plan, it's time to start the conversations . . .

Conversation #17: No Business Talk Here

I took my sixteen-year-old daughter to a client event where she rocked the room like a pro. Meeting up later, I asked what she learned; she threw out this brilliant bit of wisdom, "Did you know at business networking events, no one talks about business?" Why yes, I did know that.

So, you need to make sure you know what to talk about. Just like my daughter learned about parallel parking and had a robust discussion about dinner options . . . you need some material to rely on. This is where you take what makes you "interesting" and bring it to life. Take in the news; notice the weird and the trendy. Then start by saying hello; join the discussion; contribute to it; help ensure it's one others don't want to end.

Conversation #18: No Big Talk Here

Plan to attend one live meeting or event and engage in small talk. It's the random chatter that occupies our brains most of the time: What's new? How's the family? Where is [so and so] now? Your mission is to notice it (it happens all around you—even at the beginning of a call or video conference) and take part. Believe it or not, it is often one of the most stressful situations, simply because it's not something you tend to practice. But try it out. See what topics and approaches resonate with you. One hint: don't start practicing with your most important client ever.

Conversation #19: The Compassionate Conversation

We are in such a rush that when we hear others need a little boost, we send food, flowers, or ask about them to others. This time, take a deep breath, pick up the phone (or open an email), and check in with them. Are they doing OK? Do they need anything? Knowing they have support out there in this crazy world—building a community, where asking for help is encouraged and practiced, means a lot. Just remember, we all have those days. Being there for others is good for your own soul, too.

Conversation #20: The Pivot

This is the point when you want to move the conversation from chit-chat to something business-related. A gentle pivot. Starting with, "While we are talking, "I am wondering what you are [seeing/hearing/thinking] about ____________." Fill the blank with something smart and savvy to match who you are talking to, rather than something generic like, "What's it like to be in-house?" Ask for some ideas or guidance; expand the conversation in a way that energizes you. If you love nerding out on technical stuff, ask about it. If you are more interested in the workflow, focus on that. The key is not to try and impress; this always tends to land wrong.

Conversation #21: The Group Lunch

Sitting around a table with three to seven people causes a challenge. The conversation tends to flow from the big question at the table, to pinging back and forth with the people sitting directly next to you.

First off, please be the one who makes sure everyone knows everyone else. Use this moment of introduction to learn one thing about everyone at the table. Following up later with an email or an idea from the conversation is the key to moving these opportunities to the next stage in the progression.

A side note, these often happen at conferences. Before you sit down, introduce yourself to those you don't know. Stay off your phone and be interested in those around you. This is a great place to practice both small talk and curious conversations.

Conversation #22: The Best Ice Breaker

Once my daughter was in a meeting and the icebreaker was, "What's your favorite roof shingle color." We often refer to this as the worst icebreaker ever. Because WTF?! That being said, you need an icebreaker—but it needs to be good. Whether it's for a meeting, or just in the moment, you need a light question to ask everyone around you at a cocktail conversation. Make it something you are at least mildly interested in. If you refuse to get on an airplane, asking for a favorite international travel destination is not a good fit.

Want to know mine? I will give you one hint; it has to do with cooking (but not a recipe).

Conversation #23: End the Conversation: In Person

OK, this isn't exactly a conversation type, but we're going to call it that for the sake of the exercise. Let's admit it, getting stuck in a conversation sucks. And knowing how to move away gracefully takes some skill and practice. There are a couple popular options: grab someone else, introduce them, and politely excuse yourself; or start walking toward others as you talk—the person will follow, and you can casually excuse yourself as you go. But there's another way. Tell them you have one more quick question before you let them go, as you don't want to monopolize their time. Ask one final, short, question; then take your leave (and a quick breath of relief).

Conversation #24: End the Conversation: On the Phone

Do you know the call that goes on and on? Well, knowing how to end it gracefully is an art all its own. When the conversation wraps up, circle back to the reason for the call. You might say, "To make sure I have this clear; this is the plan to move forward..." Or, "Now that we have clarified ____________, I will circle back by email if we have additional questions." Thank them for their time and wish them a great day.

Advancing the Conversation: Connecting and Conversing on LinkedIn

LinkedIn is a powerful platform for professionals to connect and learn from one another. Joining the conversation means a variety of things, but one thing to stay away from is engaging in spam, sending cold messages, or thinking it's the way to make a pitch or sale. Instead, focus on using the posts to engage in meaningful discussions and enhancing your network of conversations on and off the platform.

Conversation #25: Joining Someone Else's Discussion

You would never walk into a cocktail party, grab a bullhorn, and expect everyone to stop and listen. Instead, you walk around and listen to the conversations already happening. Joining one, you find the natural information or idea to share. You'll use this same strategy on LinkedIn. Find a post of those you work with or around and read the comments. When you have something to share that enhances the discussion (not hijacks or makes it all about you), add a simple comment. Again, it needs to add something; "great idea" won't cut it. But if you share something along the lines of, "I do the same thing, but always point out to clients ______ and _______ to make sure they see the full strategy." Suddenly, you will be part of the discussion. Give it a try!

Conversation #26: Launching Your Own Discussion (Also Called Posting)

When you are ready, it's time for a LinkedIn post. Find a way to share where you are from or how you were trained on LinkedIn. Start with a story about how you picked your practice area, or how it picked you. Then, tell us how it impacts your work. Need some ideas? Grab that timeline and pick one story. Keep it short and simple.

Conversation #27: The Private Message

OK, you have been engaging on LinkedIn for a while, and you notice there are people who comment and engage on the same posts. You would like to get to know them and/or learn more about what they do. Better yet, they are talking about something you don't want to bore everyone with, so you want to take it offline. This is when the private message scenario works. Send a short note and ask to connect for a conversation. Please note, this is not appropriate with someone you have never engaged with, and it should not be to "sell" anything. Please don't spam everyone with this request and understand that many people ignore messages or check them infrequently. Be patient. (Also, you should make sure people you might want to work with are not sending you messages; ignoring such notes is walking away from business.)

Conversation #28: Be the Instigator

LinkedIn is a great way to spark a conversation. But you do need to know what you are getting into. For instance, I once asked for an opinion on how to start an email. Let me tell you the debate that ensued from there; it is a hotly contested topic that people are passionate about. If you can tap into a topic that is related to your work, or how you work, and you feel confident in engaging in the opinions . . . my vote is to bring it on. The best way to go about it is a one-sentence question that asks for everyone to engage. No need for a long lead-up. Keep it short and direct. Just make sure you look at all the angles—all the ways people could respond—before you post.

What to Do If . . .

Conversations come with some awkward moments. Should you continue to stalk them, leave a message, or hope they remember to call back? Should you meet by Zoom or regular phone call? Do you need to jump on a plane to go see them? What do you do when things seem to be going so well, or you're worried it's all slipping away? Sometimes worry is getting in the way of clarity. Either way, here are a few tips to hold back on overthinking and keep moving forward with your client relationships and awesome conversations.

Conversation #29: They Don't Answer . . . Leave a Voicemail

When you decide to pick up the phone rather than schedule a call, there is a chance the person won't be available. You will be forced to leave a voicemail. Since this is not 1992 (and caller ID has been invented), if you don't leave a voicemail, you get quickly placed in the stalker category. This is a conversation merely because it is your first impression or a continuation of a discussion. Do not assume they will look at the call list—nor should you assume the text transcript of your message is accurate. Make it short: name, phone number. Speak slowly enough that they can write it down. How do you know? Practice writing it yourself while speaking. Give enough information (including how much time you need), so they'll want to call back.

Conversation #30: Need a Plane, a Zoom, or an Old-Fashioned Call?

Before you buy a plane ticket, which has its place in the client development plan, take a deep breath and decide whether phone or video chat will work. Not all discussions need a face-face meeting (either in person or on Zoom), but some do—when you want to gauge the reaction, bring multiple people into the discussion, or share a document, for example.

If you want to test out your video networking, bring three to four people together for a virtual coffee. Make sure to pick something to jump start the conversation, and let it flow from there. If you invite more than four, you'll want to plan for breakout rooms. At this point, you become less of a participant and more of a facilitator. While this is my favorite position to be in, it is not for everyone, and you need to prep for the role. Know who is coming; make sure everyone is comfortable and has a place, so everyone can enjoy it.

Keep to a phone call when you need to touch base or tackle a topic that allows for a good flow of one-on-one conversation. Even better, if you can plan to take a walk and catch up with a client while you both get a smidge of fresh air.

That's it. Thirty conversations in thirty days. When you complete this challenge, you have engaged with those who work around you; with your Ideals; with prospects you are wanting to nurture—all in a careful, clever, non-sales-pitchy fashion. As you continue to maintain your curious connection, pay attention, and learn. And remember, clients want to work with real people. So, show up and be you. It will pay off exponentially (which is the long game worth playing).

One More Thing

Building a book of business and deciding to actively engage in growing incredible client relationships is all about giving you back the power in your own career. It's power built off being present, making choices, and owning your practice.

As you clear your desk and inbox, you stop tackling the nagging stuff. You begin to engage in the real projects you want—and remember the reasons you continue to practice. As you clear your mindset, the courage to take those next steps gets a little easier. You might even pick up that phone with a little pep in your step. By engaging in collaborative relationships that solve problems, rather than stir them up, you show up at the firm as a leader, rather than one more person in the long line of gripes. Most importantly, you engage in client conversations in a way that works for you, not the other guy.

As you lead from a space of curiosity and genuine conversations, we must remember this is a practice and an adjustment of your approach. Building the book of your dreams never just happens once, without needing to revisit it. This is a lifestyle change and choice.

There is one more thing to acknowledge…

You are allowed to want whatever big dream lives inside of you.

The choices of what you build and how it looks are yours.

1. You are allowed (and encouraged) to want a bigger salary.

2. You are allowed (and encouraged) to find a working schedule that works for you.

3. You are allowed (and encouraged) to want the number of clients that works for you and your practice.

4. You are allowed to want a prestigious career (and however you define this is totally cool).

5. You are allowed to want more, bigger, better. You are also allowed to want less, if that works best for you.

6. You are allowed to want to be the change in this industry.

7. You are allowed to want to help others and be the one to make it happen for them.

8. You are allowed to want to become a judge, a CEO, or the managing partner of your firm.

Dream big. Dream often. Engage in the conversations that light you up and pay attention to the ones that don't. And when you are ready, take one big, bold step toward making the dream your own reality—in a way that allows you to love your practice, work with outstanding clients, and have the life you want to live.

But before we go, grab that timeline and fill in those choices. Where have you found your power along the way? What are the active choices you are making now? Write it down and mark it with today's date. You have done the work, through challenges and choices. Continue to own your place. Celebrate it. And know I'm celebrating with you every step of the way.

Acknowledgments

There are too many people who made this project come to life to name everyone here, but as a start…

From the first conversation, I knew Ann Sheybani was going to be the one to finally get this book out of my head. From the 6 a.m. coffee and conversations, to the endless sticky notes, I am forever thankful.

To my team, and my family, for all the times I forced you into brainstorming sessions and edits—not to mention the bravery it took to point me back to the path when I was off track—so much gratitude. There would not be a book without my LinkedIn family, thank you for the incredible content that drives conversations and community; knowing we have built something far greater together means so much. And to those who helped build my law practice, so much appreciation for the endless BBQ lunches, while teaching me what excellence looks and feels like.

There would be no story without Harriet, Ruth, and Ron teaching me everything I know about building authentic client relationships, hosting amazing discussions, and holding my own when it's time to play big. And to Andrew who reminds me that a long drive with Tom Petty always puts things in perspective.

Last, but certainly not least, to my clients and the #BizDeb community, walking this path and the work you invite me to do with you each day is an honor. I can't wait to see what's next.

About the Author

Deb Feder is a business development coach, strategist, owner, and CEO of Feder Development LLC, a consulting firm focused on helping lawyers and professionals bring in consistent clients through curious, confident conversations and changing the way we view productivity for professionals.

Deb believes in simple productivity solutions. Using LinkedIn as a platform to validate and share ideas, she helps professionals engage in meaningful content and connections. For the last decade, she has committed herself to changing the way we think about work-life balance and how we tackle high-stakes work, allowing for big careers while enjoying our free time. Deb is all about dropping excuses, getting productive, and bringing in business through her Membership and Focus30 sessions.

Prior to founding Feder Development, Deb practiced corporate law for 15 years; she holds a history degree from the University of Michigan and her JD/MBA from the University of Iowa. Deb completed her coach training and certification through New Ventures West and completed the training in The Daring

Way™, which is based on the research of Dr. Brené Brown. As a contributing author to the best-selling anthology *#Networked*, Deb shares her common-sense approach to building business relationships and is a frequent speaker at conferences, podcasts, and corporate retreats on business development, productivity, networking, authenticity, and communication.

Made in the USA
Monee, IL
21 April 2024

57134745R00125